SACRED
SITES

SACRED SITES

Christian Perspectives on the Holy Land

Webster T. Patterson

Paulist Press
New York/Mahwah, N.J.

Figures 2 and 3 courtesy of Studium Biblicum Franciscanum belonging to the Franciscan Custody of the Holy Land, Jerusalem, Israel. Used with permission.

All maps are courtesy of the author.

The scripture quotations contained herein are from the New Revised Standard Version Bible © copyright 1989 by the Division of Christian Education of the National Council of the Churches of Christ in the U.S.A. Used by permission. All rights reserved.

Book design by Lynn Else
Cover design by Cynthia Dunne

Library of Congress Cataloging-in-Publication Data

Patterson, Webster T.
    Sacred sites : Christian perspectives on the Holy Land / Webster T. Patterson.
        p. cm.
    Includes bibliographcial references (p.   ).
    ISBN 0-8091-4246-5
    1. Christian antiquities—Palestine. 2. Christian shrines—Palestine. 3. Sacred space—Palestine. 4. Palestine—Antiquities. 5. Palestine—church history. I. Title.
    BR133.P3P38 2004
    263'.0425694—dc22

                                                            2003020946

Published by Paulist Press
997 Macarthur Boulevard
Mahwah, New Jersey 07430

www.paulistpress.com

Printed and bound in the
United States of America

Contents

Illustrations

*To Lorna, Tom, Jean, Suzi, Kaitlyn, Caroline,
and my extended Patterson family*

Acknowledgments

I am indebted to the many members of the Loyola College Study Tours for their inspiration and enthusiastic participation in our numerous visits to the Holy Land. Likewise, Moses Hanania and his wonderfully proficient staff at Consolidated Tours Organization, Inc., have earned my gratitude many times over for doing such a perfect job with the organizational part of our varied tours.

My appreciation is also extended to various Loyola staff and faculty. Among them, Lisa Flaherty and especially Susan Szczybor have graciously given me continued practical assistance. Andrew Ciafalo got this project underway by inviting me to submit pieces I had written for tour members to the *Catholic Review*, where they were subsequently published. Kevin Atticks also provided valuable feedback and advice. And Kate Ryan transformed my rough maps and diagrams into clear graphics.

Others to whom I owe special thanks are Fr. Lawrence Boadt, C.S.P., president of Paulist Press, who communicated his belief that this was indeed a viable work and whose suggested additions vastly improved the manuscript. To Daniel Clark, an electronics engineer and a more than kind neighbor, I owe a special debt of gratitude for technical assistance and the many hours he patiently walked us though graphics and other computer challenges.

I would also like to recognize the contributions of noted archaeologists Daniel Bahat and Fr. Jerome Murphy-O'Connor, O.P. In addition to brief but extremely helpful meetings with each of them in Jerusalem, their writings were invaluable to my own research.

I am deeply grateful to close friends who have provided support in a myriad of ways. Dr. Nina Tassi's insightful criticism and counsel throughout the long process of pulling this work together was of great value. Dr. James Buckley, his wife, Christine, Prof. Roderick Hindery, his wife Sheila, and the St. Vincent de Paul parish community also contributed ongoing insights and encouragement.

Our family has been deeply involved in this work from its inception. My son Tom (who took some of the photos for this volume) and his wife Suzi have followed its development with keen interest, encouraging me from the sidelines. Our daughter Jean and our granddaughters Kaitlyn and Caroline merit our thanks as well. They so often provided a needed respite that helped to lighten long hours of work and put everything into a very humanized perspective. Finally, the debt I owe to my wife, Lorna, is more than words can express. Not only did she take most of the photos that appear in these pages, but she gave me constant encouragement and insightful critiques. She read and reread, typed and then retyped. She prodded, cajoled, humored, and cheered me on, but most of all, when the book finally reached completion she still loved me.

Introduction

Often biblical passages have their full impact only in the context of the places where the words were spoken or where the events occurred. Concrete circumstances are essential in the history of Christianity, which is not an abstract philosophy or theory but is incarnational. The word became flesh and dwelt among us—in a definite place at a specific time in history. If one takes the time to listen, these biblical sites have something to say.

In visiting sacred sites, one's purpose is not only to try to see what Jesus saw but also to relate gospel passages to the physical context in which they took place. In our own lives we often remember events in connection with locations; these include the sights, sounds, indeed all our sensory input, at the place where the events occurred. So also it is with the episodes in the life of Christ. To place oneself at the Sea of Galilee, for example, is to evoke memories of Jesus calming the storm or to feel the crisp morning air while savoring the smell of fish sizzling on the open fire (Jn 26:9–16).

With this aim in mind, we have arranged each chapter of this book to open with essays giving background information on a particular site, followed by full biblical passages matched with photos for the practical convenience of one who is actually visiting the Holy Land. However, the book may also be useful for the "armchair traveler," affording a vicarious journey or pilgrimage to the sacred sites. Besides the scripture passages reproduced with the photographs, additional references, maps, and other information are provided.

Fine guidebooks on the Holy Land abound; this is not another. Rather it is highly selective, focusing on the more authentic and significant biblical sites. The book aims to combine theology, scripture, archaeology, and history in an easily readable style. Developing the background knowledge and spiritual insights of the average Christian visitor is its obvious and underlying objective.

The book begins in chapter 1 with Galilee as it is now and as it was at the time of Christ. Special effort is made to create a vivid description of the area so that readers can sense the atmosphere—the sights, the smells, the sounds—and feel present. Following Galilee, chapter 2, on Jerusalem, concentrates on that one square mile within the high-walled battlements of the Old City, the area that is still the foremost sacred city to much of the world's population.

Jesus' hidden years, covered in chapter 3, involve both Bethlehem and Nazareth. Giving not only the background and history of the two main basilicas, the Nativity and the Annunciation, the chapter also positions these two sites within the cultural context that surrounded Christ's thirty years in Nazareth. Chapter 4 explores the Greco-Roman world in which Jesus lived and ministered, beginning with Caesarea Maritima, Herod the Great's famous seaport on the Mediterranean. Leaning heavily on Luke's Acts of the Apostles, chapter 5 attempts to search out the sites frequented by the apostles and the first Jewish Christians after the ascension.

The book is the product of the author's extensive and unique personal experience. It combines my career as a theologian and college professor with my role as leader of many study tours to the Holy Land. The need for a volume such as this became apparent as a result of my work with these learning groups. Unable to find appropriate reading material for tour participants, I began to write articles that would give them the knowledge needed for a more in-depth travel experience. Most of these articles were eventually published by Baltimore's *Catholic Review*.

Writings on the Holy Land frequently tend to be overly pietistic on the one hand, or too heavily laden with scholarship on the other. The former often disregard the reality of current solid research and treat all Holy Land sites, however doubtful, as equally worthy of veneration. The latter, though valuable, can be so academic that the average reader is left cold. We attempt to avoid both extremes by creating a work that incorporates scholarship with a presentation that is readable, accurate, and reverent. This is the ambiance of the work—an effort to bring the reader closer to the reality reflected in the gospel.

G. K. Chesterton once observed, "It is not only the visible but the invisible deeper associations of the sacred sites which have drawn hundreds of millions to visit the Holy Land down through the ages." Perhaps it is for this reason that this small book is the culmination of the author's many years of personal experience in teaching and leading study tours. A deep love for the area where God chose to become man has been a lifelong focus. It is hoped that those who use this book will find that it enriches their visit to the sacred sites or helps them relive a previous experience there.

Chapter I
GALILEE

Photo by Lorna Patterson

Fig. 1 Sea of Galilee. The Sea of Galilee is truly the lake of Jesus. He walked on its waters. He spoke by its shores. He made it his home after leaving Nazareth. This scene looks east across the lake from a hill near Capernaum, the traditional Mount of Beatitudes.

Map 1
THE HOLY LAND AT THE TIME OF CHRIST

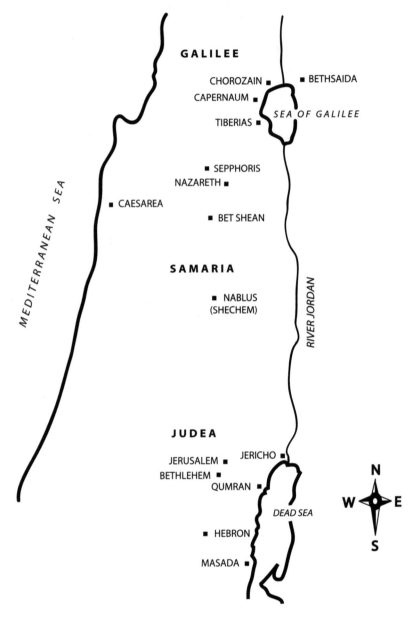

GALILEE

CHOROZAIN ■   ■ BETHSAIDA

CAPERNAUM ■

SEA OF GALILEE

TIBERIAS ■

MEDITERRANEAN SEA

■ SEPPHORIS

NAZARETH ■

■ CAESAREA

■ BET SHEAN

SAMARIA

■ NABLUS
(SHECHEM)

RIVER JORDAN

JUDEA

JERICHO ■

JERUSALEM ■

BETHLEHEM ■

QUMRAN ■

N
W ✦ E
S

DEAD SEA

■ HEBRON

MASADA ■

Map 2
LAKESIDE PORTS OF THE GOSPELS

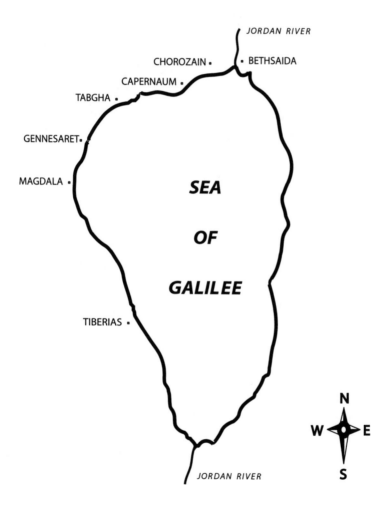

Map 3
THE MINISTRY OF JESUS

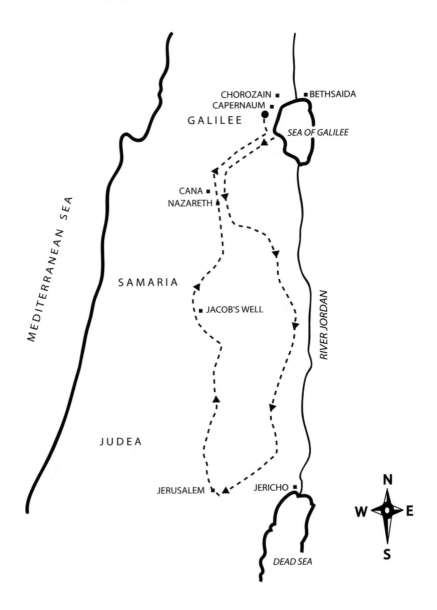

A Panoramic View: Sea of Galilee

Most visitors to the Holy Land approach the Sea of Galilee from the west, and they catch their first view from high in the hills. A mountain road curves sharply, when suddenly the lake below appears—an azure blue ribbon nestled in the mountains. This is the Sea of Galilee, a heart-shaped lake seven miles wide and thirteen long.

Across the lake, straight to the east, the towering cliffs of the Golan Heights plunge down into the shimmering blue-green waters. The lake lies calm without a ripple. Galilee is sleeping. Under the dying sun's rays, Golan's high bluffs turn from scorched brown to yellow and golden red.

Galilee. Even the sound is melodious—like the splashing of waves washing over the rocky beach and then receding. To fall asleep lulled by that rhythmic music is a good reason to lodge on Galilee's lakeside near the water's edge. With waves lapping outside an open window, it is not hard to imagine Christ walking on these same waters or his apostles plying the lake for an early morning's catch. A squall may arise suddenly during the night to heighten the experience.

Although the Sea of Galilee is a lake of enchanting beauty, it can display a variety of moods almost at a given moment. Even without warning sometimes fierce winds sweep down from Mount Hermon in the North, lashing the rolling waves into a frenzy. At those times, the gospel scene of Christ calming the storm at sea takes on a new dimension.

The western side of the lake today is much like it was when Jesus walked these shores; if anything it was more populous then than it is now. According to Jewish historian Flavius Josephus and other ancient sources, hundreds of fishing vessels crisscrossed its waters, transporting travelers, tradesmen, and fishermen back and forth between fishing ports.[1] What makes this lake so unique is that it is a little inland sea sunk in a tropical trench seven hundred feet below sea level. The mountains around it enjoy a temperate climate; the lake itself is subtropical, with shores lined with palms, bamboo, and banana trees. Unlike the bitter salt water of the Dead Sea, the waters of the Sea of Galilee are clear and fresh.[2]

Some areas around the north end of the lake are still desolate, as they were in the time of Christ, especially around Bethsaida and Chorozain, recalling those chilling words of Jesus reproaching them for their lack of faith: "Woe to you Chorozain! Woe to you Bethsaida!...I tell you on the day of judgment it will be more tolerable for Tyre and Sidon than for you" (Mt 11:21–22). Near the water's edge in this region rise mounds of black basalt, like monuments reminding one of Christ's stinging words. Actually Bethsaida and Chorozain are only three miles apart, separated by the Jordan River, which flows into the Sea of Galilee from the foothills of Mount Hermon.

Bethsaida: Lost and Then Found

The feeding of the five thousand took place near Bethsaida (Lk 9:12–17). Jesus cured a blind man in the city itself (Mk 8:22–25). Then, near Bethsaida, we find Jesus walking on the water after the multiplication of loaves (Mk 6:22–45). Bethsaida is mentioned more often than any other city in the New Testament except Jerusalem and Capernaum. Yet the location of the site somehow got lost in history. Some have even called it the city that disappeared, because early Christian pilgrims tried to find it but did not know where to look— somewhere on the northeastern end of the Sea of Galilee, but exactly where nobody knew.[3]

Bethsaida in the tenth century B.C. was the main city of a small kingdom called Geshur. Historically it appears in the Egyptian Tel el-Amarna letters, diplomatic correspondence (cuneiform tablets) between the Pharaoh Akhenaten (1352–1338 B.C.) and his vassals in

Palestine. The city came into the hands of Philip, son of Herod the Great, when the latter died in 4 B.C. It is mentioned by Josephus (Antiquities 8:26) but did not survive the Jewish rebellion against Rome (A.D. 67). After that the exact location of Bethsaida was lost—perhaps due to the rise of the lake level, leaving the fishing village submerged under water today. This is the theory of Mendel Nun, a resident of Kibbutz Ein Gev, a modern fishing village on the southeastern shore. Although not a professional archaeologist, Nun has spent twenty-five years exploring the shores all around the lake.

However, recently an alternative explanation has been given by archaeologists excavating at a site a mile and a half inland from the lakeshore—to be sure, an unlikely place for a fishing village. Apparently earthquakes and mudslides extended the shoreline southward, leaving the site of Bethsaida separated from its original location. In the ruins of this city, fishhooks, weights for fishing nets, anchors, and a seal depicting fishermen throwing nets into the sea were found.[4]

Peter, Andrew, and Philip originally came from Bethsaida. Why they left to settle in Capernaum is not clear. Perhaps the move was for economic reasons, that is, to avoid paying the customs tax when crossing over the border from Bethsaida to Capernaum. Fishermen needed to be near the place where fish were preserved, a necessity in the heat of Galilee. In the absence of refrigeration fish do not do well in such a climate, so salting or pickling was a real need. Rather than continually crossing the border (and paying the tax), it was much cheaper just to live at Capernaum near Magdala, where the fish salting industry was located.

Fishing is still an important occupation of the Sea of Galilee, which is kept well stocked for the fishermen who sail its waters. Kibbutz Ein Gev, on the eastern side below the Golan Heights, is a modern fishing town specializing in a kind of perch called St. Peter's fish. In the time of Christ the sea was ringed with harbors from which boats like the one preserved at Kibbutz Nof Ginosar set forth. This first-century boat was discovered recently in the mud near the kibbutz when the lake was low. Most likely it is the same type of boat used by Christ and his apostles.[5]

Chorozain: A Town with a View

Only three miles from Bethsaida lies the town of Chorozain, on a hilltop above Capernaum with a panoramic view of Galilee's north end. From all that is known archaeologically, it appears that Chorozain was one of those cities founded by the influx of Jews. They came into Galilee following the defeat of two revolts against Rome—the first Jewish revolt that ended in A.D. 70 and the second that ended in A.D. 135. As the expelled Jews moved north, they founded many new towns and villages that prospered in and around Galilee. At least sixteen of them were around the shores of the Sea of Galilee itself. Obviously there was more coming and going over the lake in the time of Jesus than there is today.

In rabbinical writings of the third and fourth centuries, Chorozain is identified as one of the many "medium-sized towns" in Palestine. The site was first discovered by a Dutch officer who traveled there in the middle of the nineteenth century. While looking for ancient synagogues in 1905, two German scholars, Heinrich Kohl and Carl Watzinger, found the remains of one at Chorozain. Excavations in modern times began in the 1960s, when it was decided to include Chorozain in Israel's national park system. Since then much work has been done to restore the site, especially the synagogue.

All the buildings in Chorozain are built of hard black basalt, a volcanic rock that abounds in the area. Prominent in the city's center, the synagogue was also constructed from this stone. While the Jerusalem Temple had been the house of God, the synagogue in Chorozain was the house of the people, an integral part of their community life. It was a masterpiece of stonework—a jewel in the middle of the city.[6]

Magdala: Home of Mary Magdalene

Although not mentioned explicitly in the New Testament, Magdala is one of those prosperous temple fishing ports lining the western shores of the lake. Its Greek name, *Tracheae*, means "the place for salting fish," a clue indicating the main occupation of the town.

Even in the early days of Christianity, Magdala was identified as the hometown of Mary Magdalene. Many pilgrims went there to honor her, and a church was built on the traditional site of her house. In the seventh century it was destroyed but then rebuilt during the Crusader period. The site has been in ruins since the thirteenth century.[7]

About four miles north of Tiberias, a white-domed building marks the site of Magdala, with the ruins of the ancient town surrounding it. Since 1973, archaeological activity under the direction of the Franciscan Fathers has uncovered the remains of a Jewish town of the first century with paved streets, a villa, and shops. The ruins of a Byzantine monastery have also been discovered.

It should be mentioned that during the Jewish wars against the Romans (A.D. 67–70), Magdala was the main center of Jewish rebels in the area. At that time Flavius Josephus was the Jewish commander, though he later went over to the Roman side. After a very long siege the Romans entered, massacring the town's inhabitants and destroying its fishing fleet. Slowly the town struggled to its feet and again became a center of Jewish life.

Jesus spent much of his ministry traversing the western shore and entering synagogues where he felt at home. This was the physical context of his life, which was that of a Palestinian Jew. Often walking the roads and hills of the area he came to love its natural beauty; this is reflected time and time again in the pages of the gospel. Especially was this true of the region around Gennesaret, near his home base, Capernaum.

Gennesaret: Galilee's Garden Spot

At the northwest corner of Galilee was the garden spot described by Flavius Josephus in glowing terms: "The country which lies against the lake has the name Gennesaret. Its soil is so fruitful that all kinds of trees can grow upon it, walnuts palm trees, fig trees, olives and grapes."[8]

Unfortunately, the region underwent a long period of destruction and neglect during the Turkish occupation. Forests were cut down. Crops were abandoned. Fields once fertile were allowed to lie fallow. But the previous century has seen a revival; restoration is underway, so that it now begins to look as it must have appeared at the time of Christ. Especially in the spring, the area is ablaze with color: flower-decked meadows, golden fields of barley, vineyards laden with purple grapes, all interspersed with olive groves and clumps of pines woven into the fabric of the land.

Today, along the shore of the lake the visitor encounters much the same kind of activity that Jesus viewed in his time. Fishing boats pull up on the rocky shore in the early morning. Fishermen can still be seen mending nets and hanging them in the trees. New, of course, are the eucalyptus trees, imported from Australia in the last century. But an overview of the whole Sea of Galilee is best begun with a trip to Capernaum, the town Jesus made his home for three years after leaving Nazareth. Either by car or by boat, the trip can be made from Tiberias, the only large town on the lake today.

Although Tiberias does not figure in the story of Jesus, it did exist in his time, having been founded in A.D. 22 by Herod Antipas, the Herod who is mentioned in the gospel narrative of Christ's passion. After the destruction of Jerusalem (A.D. 70), the town became a center of Jewish learning famous in connection with rabbinical writings (e.g., the Mishnah and the Talmud). Outside the city are the Horns of Hattin, where the Muslim forces of Saladin defeated the Crusaders in A.D. 1187.

At Tiberias one may board a boat modeled after a first-century fishing boat (called the "Jesus boat") discovered on the lake bottom in the 1980s. About halfway out into the lake the boat's motor is cut off, leaving the small craft to drift gently in the rolling waves. Some passengers read a passage from the New Testament depicting Christ on these same waters. Others sit in silent contemplation. After awhile the boat goes on to arrive at the wooded peninsula where the ruins lie half-hidden among the eucalyptus trees. This is Capernaum, the town Jesus made his headquarters during the three years of his public life. After being rejected at Nazareth, he made it his home or "his own town" in the words of Matthew (Mt 9:1).

Capernaum: The Town of Jesus

Why Jesus chose Capernaum is not certain. As far as it is known, the town had no advantages over similar villages in Galilee. Possibly he chose it because this is where Peter and Andrew and other of his first disciples lived. Apparently it was not a wealthy town, which can be inferred from the fact that a Roman centurion had to finance the building of its synagogue. When the townspeople "came to Jesus they appealed to him earnestly, saying, 'He is worthy of having you do this for him, for he loves our people, and it is he who built our synagogue for us'" (Lk 7:4–5). Capernaum was the center of several commercial routes and was located on the border of two provinces, Galilee and Gaulanitis, a town with its own customs station as well as a garrison under a centurion. It was here that Matthew, the customs collector, had his seat of operation. And here the gathering of Jesus' first disciples took place. This was the beginning of what later came to be called the *ecclesia* or church.

In Hebrew, *kefar* means town or village; Nahum was a minor prophet of the Old Testament. So the name *Cephar Naum* means "the village of Nahum." Otherwise, little is known about its origin except that after the time of Jesus, an early Jewish Christian community lived there—"a continuing Christian presence attested to both archaeologically and textually."[9]

Today at the gate-entrance to the ruins a prominent sign greets the visitor: "CAPHARNAUM: THE TOWN OF JESUS." Where this entrance actually was is not known. The center of the town with its synagogue is only a few yards ahead; Jesus must have passed by many times. Somewhere near here he chose his first apostles: "As Jesus passed along the Sea of Galilee, he saw Simon and his brother Andrew casting a net into the sea....As he went a little farther, he saw James son of Zebedee and his brother John...and they left their father Zebedee...and followed him...to Capernaum" (Mk 1:16–21). In no other area did Christ give so many discourses or work so many miracles. Mark's first chapter enumerates one healing episode after another, which inspired crowds to follow Jesus everywhere. Among these narratives are the well-known cures of the paralytic and of Peter's mother-in-law (Mt 1:20).

Obviously Capernaum played a major role in the beginnings of Christianity. Today it has two significant features: the impressive limestone synagogue and the house of Saint Peter. They have been the objects of controversy among archaeologists, though some consensus now seems to prevail regarding both, especially in the area of dating. At one time, some held that Capernaum's synagogue dates from the first or second century. But the general thinking today is that it could not have been built before the second half of the fourth century. This reasoning is attributed partly to the large cache of dated coins and pottery found sealed beneath the building.

Nevertheless, according to Jewish custom, a new synagogue was built on the foundation of the old; such seems to have been the case there.[10] In some areas, remains of the black basalt foundation can be seen under the white limestone structure—the foundation of the synagogue with which Jesus was familiar and attended on the Sabbath (Mk 1:21). He would have known it well.

Due to its raised position and ornate decoration it dominated the entire town. Capernaum's synagogue is considered one of the grandest if not the best in all Galilee. The structure was large, with a generous courtyard outside to the east for community gatherings. Inside, stone benches were wrapped around the walls, stressing the original meaning of the word *synagogue* as a place for the assembly to hear the reading of the Torah, not a place of worship.

The synagogue one sees today in Capernaum is believed to have been built about the fourth century A.D., and its ruins are remarkably well preserved. When the city degenerated in the sixth century A.D., the building fell into ruins and was covered with debris. In the 1880s the Franciscans purchased the site, excavated the ruins, and partially restored the synagogue.

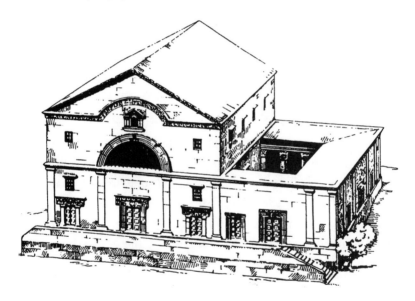

Fig. 2 Hypothetical reconstruction of the synagogue. Shown is a reconstruction of the white fourth-century synagogue built on a raised podium dominating the ruins of Capernaum. Long before recent excavations began, scholars had suggested that the synagogue actually visited by Jesus was buried under this monumental fourth-century structure, but hardly any believed it could ever be proved—including the famous archaeologist W. F. Albright. However, beginning in 1969, Franciscan archaeologists Corbo and Loffreda cut several trenches around this synagogue, exposing what lay beneath. Result: Beneath was a very large stone pavement of the first century A.D. belonging to the long-sought-after synagogue built by the Roman centurion and visited by Jesus (Loffreda, *Recovering Capernaum*, p. 35).

The Origin of the Synagogue

At this point it might be well to reflect on the origin of the synagogue in Israelite history, which is somewhat shrouded in mystery. The more common opinion is that the synagogue as an institution began during the Babylonian exile, when the Jewish people were far from their destroyed Temple in Jerusalem. It is thought that Ezra brought it to Palestine after the return from exile. Another opinion is that the synagogue was started by Ezra and Nehemiah as a means to strengthen their government. Still another opinion is that the synagogue is much older, going back before the time of the destruction of the Temple, as far back as Josiah, or perhaps even to the period of King Jehoshaphat, when levites and priests went throughout the land of Judah to teach the law (2 Chron 17:7–9).

Papyri have been found that indicate the existence of synagogues in Egypt in the third century B.C. At the time of Jesus there were synagogues throughout the civilized world to care for the needs of the diaspora or exiled Jews. Each village had its *synagogue*, a term that stands for the congregation and the place of their meeting. The synagogue was not a temple in the sense of priestly celebration; there was no altar. It was a hall, a meeting place for prayer and song. Its main feature was and is today a tabernacle or ark that held the scrolls of the Law—the Torah. There was a platform or pulpit for the reader; the congregation sat on benches or stools. The architecture of the synagogue was simple and was adapted to the local style.

The House of Peter

Between the synagogue and the lake is the site venerated as the house of Saint Peter, where Jesus may have lodged (Mt 5:20). To the casual visitor it looks disappointing, simply a chaotic mass of black basalt walls or the ruins of them. What is certain is that they are remains of the houses of the first century, walls that would have been familiar to Jesus. Here the structures appear in clusters, each surrounding a courtyard. In one group stands a house unlike all the others—evidence that it was public and very special.

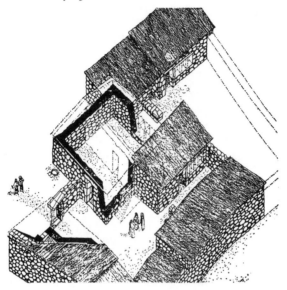

Fig. 3 Hypothetical reconstruction of Peter's house. The house of Saint Peter often mentioned in the Synoptic Gospels was rediscovered in 1968 under the foundations of the octagonal Byzantine church of the fifth century, about ninety yards south of the synagogue. The artist's reconstruction shows Peter's house off an L-shaped courtyard. Dwellings of this time (first century A.D.) were characterized by small thatched-roofed rooms clustered around courtyards (Loffreda 1990, 53).

Of course, identification of the site with the owner is not possible. But archaeologist Fr. Jerome Murphy-O'Connor has observed, "The evidence of consistent veneration in the pre-Constantian period demands an explanation." According to Murphy-O'Connor, the development of this first-century site into a fully recognized church in Byzantine times indicates a strong tradition connecting this place with Peter and the activity of Jesus in Capernaum.[11]

The contribution of archaeology to this site might be summed up by saying that evidence dating from the first century A.D. was discovered in a room venerated by early Jewish Christians. The Christian character of this evidence is clear from graffiti discovered on the walls of the house believed to be that of Peter: Jesus is called the Lord, Christ, the Most High, God. Some liturgical expressions such as *Amen* and *Kyrie eleison* are also present. The plurality of languages found (Aramaic, Greek, Latin) suggests that the site was visited not simply by local worshipers but by pilgrims as well.[12]

This is confirmed by the diary of the nun Egeria, who visited the site in the fourth century. She describes the house of Peter in these terms: "The house of the prince of the Apostles (St. Peter) in Capharnaum was changed into a church; the walls, however (of that house) are still standing as they were (in the past)." Egeria does not speak of a common church but of a house changed into a church. To stress the point, Egeria underscores the fact that the walls of the old house were still standing as in the past.[13]

So by the fourth and fifth centuries a complex picture had emerged: two public buildings, a synagogue and a church, close together. Visitors are sometimes puzzled by finding a Jewish synagogue and a Christian shrine almost side by side. To be sure, the location of the buildings was determined by the sacredness of both sites; the Byzantine church was built to perpetuate the exact location of Peter's house; the fourth-century white synagogue rose on the remains of one older—the one dating from the time of Jesus whose foundations have been discovered. Recent excavations thus have shed a new light on the biblical site of Capernaum. A large portion of the living quarters were exposed, and the public buildings—namely, the synagogue and the octagonal church—over the traditional house of Peter were set again in the physical and historical contexts.[14]

The Mount of Beatitudes

From Capernaum one can view a long sloping hill that has come to be called the Mount of Beatitudes. Although there is no archaeological evidence to confirm accuracy of the area, the Franciscan Sisters have built there an octagonal church and a hospice for pilgrims. Certainly the site is one of the most beautiful in the Holy Land. From its height one can absorb the marvelous panorama of the whole Sea of Galilee, virtually every place where Jesus lived and worked during his public ministry.

Fig. 4 Pottery from the house of Peter. In the first-century house venerated by early Jewish Christians archaeologists discovered fragments of Herodian lamps that were embedded in white plastered pavements. More Herodian lamps were found along the inner walls. The lamps can be dated typologically in the second half of the first century A.D. and certainly not later than the beginning of the second century. This is the only case in which a room with plastered pavements and walls has been found in Capernaum, in spite of the fact that a very large portion of the ancient village has been brought to light. A conclusion is that this room—along with other evidence—was used for community gatherings as early as the third quarter of the first century A.D.

Later on, the site was covered by a church as described by the pilgrim nun Egeria in the latter part of the fourth century. On this church-house a Byzantine church was constructed—octagonal in shape—in the fifth century. All of these layers have been uncovered and identified by Franciscan archaeologists since the 1960s, as documented and illustrated by Fr. Stanislao Loffreda, O.F.M., in his booklet, *Recovering Capernaum* (p. 57).

Although lacking archaeological interest, the Mount of Beatitudes affords an unparalleled view so well described by the late British travel writer H. V. Morton:

> The Sea of Galilee, even in its desolation, breathes an exquisite peace and beauty that surpass anything in the land. The landscape has altered in detail since Jesus made

his home in Capernaum, but the broad outline has not
changed. The hills are the hills He looked upon, the lights
and the shadows, that turn the Gergesene Heights to gold
and purple, the little breezes that whip the lake into white-
ness, the blue water that fades into the milky green where
the Jordan enters at the north; none of these has changed.
These are the things Jesus looked upon and loved when he
lived in Galilee.[15]

The name "Mount of Beatitudes" is derived from Matthew's version of the location of this famous discourse. Luke has called it "the
sermon on the plain." An attempt to reconcile the two locations in a
literal sense is a fundamentalist approach called *concordism*. More
knowledge about the semitic mentality and its mode of expression—
which is Matthew's—is needed to understand the use of symbolic parallelism that runs throughout the Gospel of Matthew. Also to be
remembered is that discourse was not delivered all at one time, but is
a combination of teachings given at different places on different occasions. Matthew's love of parallelism, a favorite Jewish or semitic literary device, is well known. For instance, just as Moses promulgated the
Old Law on Mount Sinai, so Jesus presents the New Law on the
Mount of Beatitudes.

Below this hill, early Christians often went to a place called the
Heptapegon (or Tabgha), a grassy area with seven springs. In the
fourth century, the pilgrim Egeria left this description:

Not far [from Capernaum] are to be seen some stone steps
upon which stood the Lord. There on the lake shore is a
grassy plain having plenty of hay and many palm trees and
beside them seven springs, each having unending water in
which plain the Lord fed the crowd with five loaves and two
fishes. Truly, the stone on which the Lord placed the bread
has become an altar....Past the walls of this church goes the

public highway on which the apostle Matthew had his place of custom.[16]

From Egeria's account in the 380s it is clear that already early Christians were going to the area called Tabgha and revering it as the site of the feeding of the five thousand. According to John's Gospel (6:1–14), the multiplication of loaves and fishes actually took place on the other side of the lake. However, the event is commemorated in the Benedictine Church of the Multiplication located near Capernaum. It preserves remains of earlier churches built on the site, including one of the most beautiful mosaic floors in the Holy Land. Most prominent in the sanctuary is the ancient stone altar before which is the celebrated mosaic of the two fishes flanking a basket of bread.

The Multiplication of the Loaves

To catch the vividness of the following episode, it helps to put it in the historical present tense. As narrated in John's Gospel, Jesus boards a boat with his disciples in Capernaum, landing on the eastern shore where the crowd has followed. After Jesus feeds the multitude miraculously, their unbridled enthusiasm prompts them to make him king. Jesus escapes alone into the mountains to pray; meanwhile

> When evening came, his disciples went down to the sea, got into a boat, and started across the sea to Capernaum. It was now dark, and Jesus had not yet come to them. The sea became rough because a strong wind was blowing. When they had rowed north about three or four miles, they saw Jesus walking on the sea..., and they were terrified. But he said to them, "It is I; do not be afraid." Then they wanted to take him into the boat, and immediately the boat reached the land toward which they were going. (Jn 6:16–21)

Upon landing, the crowd challenges him, "Rabbi, when did you come here?" (Jn 6:25). Jesus replies that they seek him not because they saw signs but because they ate of the loaves; then begins his discourse on the bread of life (Jn 6:25–29).

Jesus challenges the faith of his listeners, separating those who truly believe in him from those who do not. Although the subject matter begins with bread, the dialogue leads quickly into the difference between the manna from heaven given by Moses in the desert to belief in himself: "I am the living bread that came down from heaven. Whoever eats of this bread will live forever; and the bread that I will give for the life of the world is my flesh" (Jn 6:51). This is a hard saying. The crowd murmurs and some walk away. How can this man give us his flesh to eat? So Jesus asks the twelve, "'Do you also wish to go away?' Simon Peter answered him, 'Lord to whom can we go? You have the words of eternal life. We have come to believe that you are the Holy One of God'" (Jn 6:67–69).

Peter did not understand the "how" of Christ's saying any more than did the rest. But he truly believed. This was the response Jesus sought. Although often acting precipitously, Peter came forth this time with the right answer. It is clear that those who walked away understood Jesus in a literal sense. But what Jesus really meant is evident from the fact that he repeated the same words at least seven times, not explaining it away as a mere figure of speech but foreshadowing his real presence in the Eucharist. "Truly, I tell you, unless you eat the flesh of the Son of Man and drink his blood, you will have no life in you. Those who eat my flesh and drink my blood have eternal life, and I will raise them up on the last day; for my flesh is true food and my blood is true drink" (Jn 6:53–55).

Jesus' Resurrection Appearance

Another episode that took place on the lake near Capernaum was Jesus' appearance to the apostles after the resurrection when he served them breakfast. As narrated by John, the scene is deeply and appealingly human. By a charcoal fire on the beach, with fish sizzling on the coals, "Jesus said to them, 'Come and have breakfast!'...Jesus came and took the bread and gave it to them, and did the same with the fish" (Jn 21:12–13). After they had eaten, Jesus took Peter aside and asked him three times, "Simon, son of John, do you love me more than these?" Peter replies, "Yes, Lord, you know that I love you" (Jn 21:15). Peter was deeply hurt and humbled, remembering that it was by another charcoal fire that he denied Jesus three times. Thus, on the lake close to where the first apostles were chosen, another major milestone in the early development of the church is taken. Peter is given responsibility for the flock— the first shepherd appointed to care for the church: "Feed my lambs."

The Galilee where Jesus lived and labored and Galilee today are both similar and different. The lake with fishermen still plying its waters, surrounded by verdant fields, quiet villages, and the well-worn heights of the Golan surely provide the same vistas experienced by Christ in the first century. But the influences of modern civilization have also crept closer, bringing with them the high-rise resort hotels in Tiberias that pierce the once-tranquil rural countryside. One can still absorb and be profoundly inspired by the sites of the gospel scenes; however, times have changed, and one senses that even in Galilee the third millennium has arrived.

Sermon on the Mount: The Beatitudes

When Jesus saw the crowds, he went up the mountain; and after he sat down, his disciples came to him. Then he began to speak, and taught them, saying:

> "Blessed are the poor in spirit,
> for theirs is the kingdom of heaven.
>
> Blessed are those who mourn,
> for they will be comforted.
>
> Blessed are the meek,
> for they will inherit the earth.
>
> Blessed are those who hunger and thirst for justice,*
> for they will be filled.
>
> Blessed are the merciful,
> for they will receive mercy.
>
> Blessed are the pure in heart,
> for they will see God.
>
> Blessed are the peacemakers,
> for they will be called children of God.
>
> Blessed are those who are persecuted for justice's* sake,
> for theirs is the kingdom of heaven.
>
> Blessed are you when people revile you and persecute you and utter all kinds of evil against you falsely on my account. Rejoice and be glad, for your reward is great in heaven, for in the same way they persecuted the prophets who were before you." (Mt 5:1-12)

*The word *justice* has been substituted for the NRSV version *righteousness.*

Photo by Lorna Patterson

Fig. 5 "Mount" of Beatitudes. No archaeological evidence can prove that this hill seen from the Sea of Galilee is the "mount" Matthew refers to as the site where Jesus discoursed on the eight beatitudes (Mt 5:1–10). Luke refers to it as the "level place" (Lk 6:17). But since this "mount" is the closest one to Capernaum, Matthew's hometown, it is possible he knew.

Photo by Lorna Patterson

Fig. 6 Chapel of the Franciscan Sisters. The octagonal chapel built by the Italian Franciscan Sisters commands a magnificent panoramic view of the whole Sea of Galilee.

Capernaum

Now when Jesus heard that John had been arrested, he withdrew to Galilee. He left Nazareth and made his home in Capernaum by the sea, in the territory of Zebulun and Naphtali, so that what had been spoken through the prophet Isaiah might be fulfilled:

> "Land of Zebulun, land of Naphtali
> on the road by the sea, across the
> Jordan, Galilee of the Gentiles—
> the people who sat in darkness
> have seen a great light
> and for those who sat in the region
> and shadow of death
> light has dawned."

From that time Jesus began to proclaim, "Repent, for the kingdom of heaven has come near."

As he walked by the Sea of Galilee, he saw two brothers, Simon, who is called Peter, and Andrew his brother, casting a net into the sea— for they were fishermen. And he said to them, "Follow me, and I will make you fish for people." Immediately they left their nets and followed him. As he went from there, he saw two other brothers, James son of Zebedee and his brother John, in the boat with their father Zebedee, mending their nets, and he called them. Immediately they left the boat and their father, and followed him. (Mt 4:12-22)

When he entered Capernaum, a centurion came to him, appealing to him and saying, "Lord, my servant is lying at home paralyzed, in terrible distress." And he said to him, "I will come and cure him." The centurion said, "Lord, I am not worthy to have you come under my roof, but only speak the word, and my servant will be healed. For I also am a man under authority, with soldiers under me; and I say to one, 'Go,' and he goes, and to another, 'Come,' and he comes, and to my slave, 'Do this,' and the slave does it." When Jesus heard him, he was amazed and said to those who followed him, "Truly, I tell you, in no one in Israel have I found such faith. I tell you, many will come from the east and west and will eat with Abraham and Isaac and Jacob in the kingdom of heaven, while the heirs of the kingdom will be thrown into the outer darkness, where there will be weeping and gnashing of teeth." And to the centurion Jesus said,

"God; let it be done to you according to your faith." And the servant was healed in that hour. (Mt 8:5–13)

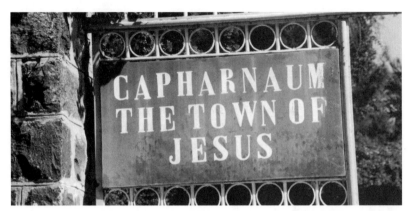

Photo by Lorna Patterson

Fig. 7 Sign from town of Capernaum. "He left Nazareth and made his home in Capernaum by the sea," says Matthew (5:12). Since 1894 the site has been owned and excavated by the Franciscans Fathers, custodians of the Holy Land's sacred sites.

Photo by Lorna Patterson

Fig. 8 Fishermen. Near here Jesus called his first disciples, who were fishermen. As seen in the recent photo, fishermen still bring in their early morning catch as they did in biblical times.

Jesus Heals in the Synagogue and Peter's House

They went to Capernaum; and when the sabbath came, he entered the synagogue and taught. They were astounded at his teaching, for he taught them as one having authority, and not as the scribes. Just then there was in their synagogue a man with an unclean spirit, and he cried out, "What have you to do with us, Jesus of Nazareth? Have you come to destroy us? I know what you are, the Holy One of God." But Jesus rebuked him, saying, "Be silent and come out of him!" And the unclean spirit, convulsing him and crying with a loud voice, came out of him. They were all amazed, and they kept on asking one another, "What is this? A new teaching—with authority! He commands even the unclean spirits, and they obey him." At once his fame began to spread throughout the surrounding region of Galilee.

As soon as they left the synagogue, they entered the house of Simon and Andrew, with James and John. Now Simon's mother-in-law was in bed with a fever, and they told him about her at once. He came and took her by the hand and lifted her up. Then the fever left her, and she began to serve them....

When he returned to Capernaum after some days, it was reported that he was at home. So many gathered around that there was no longer room for them, not even in front of the door; and he was speaking the word to them. Then some people came, bringing to him a paralyzed man, carried by four of them. And when they could not bring him to Jesus because of the crowd, they removed the roof above him; and after having dug through it, they let down the mat on which the paralytic lay. When Jesus saw their faith, he said to the paralytic, "Son, your sins are forgiven." Now some of the scribes were sitting there, questioning in their hearts. "Why does this fellow speak in this way? It is blasphemy! Who can forgive sins but God alone?" At once Jesus perceived in his spirit that they were discussing these questions among themselves; and he said to them, "Why do you raise such questions in your hearts? Which is easier to say to the paralytic—'Your sins are forgiven,' or to say, 'Stand up, take your mat and walk'? But so that you may know that the Son of Man has authority on earth to forgive sins"—he said to the paralytic—"I say to you, stand up, take your mat, and go to your home." And he stood up, and immediately took the mat and went out before all of them; so that they were all amazed and glorified God, saying, "We have never seen anything like this!" (Mk 1:21-31, 2:1-12)

Fig. 9 Ruins at Capernaum. "When the sabbath came, he entered the synagogue and taught," as Mark related (Mk 1:21). These restored ruins dominate Capernaum today. Although these remains date from the late fourth century A.D., archaeologists show that they stand on the foundation of an earlier first-century synagogue, most likely the same one Jesus entered on the Sabbath.

Fig. 10 Excavated walls at Capernaum. Depicted are first-century excavated walls Jesus would have known. One house was revered as Peter's home, from evidence left by early Christian pilgrims.

The Storm at Sea

Now when Jesus saw great crowds around him, he gave orders to go over to the other side. A scribe then approached and said, "Teacher, I will follow you wherever you go." And Jesus said to him, "Foxes have holes, and birds of the air have nests; but the Son of Man has nowhere to lay his head." Another of his disciples said to him, "Lord, first let me go and bury my father." But Jesus said to him, "Follow me, and let the dead bury their own dead."

And when he got into the boat, his disciples followed him. A windstorm arose on the sea, so great that the boat was being swamped by the waves; but he was asleep. And they went and woke him up, saying, "Lord, save us! We are perishing!" And he said to them, "Why are you afraid, you of little faith?" Then he got up and rebuked the winds and the sea; and there was a dead calm. They were amazed, saying, "What sort of man is this, that even the winds and the sea obey him?"

When he came to the other side, to the country of the Gadarenes, two demoniacs coming out of the tombs met him. They were so fierce that no one could pass that way. Suddenly they shouted, "What have you to do with us, Son of God? Have you come here to torment us before the time?" Now a large herd of swine was feeding at some distance from them. The demons begged him, "If you cast us out, send us into the herd of swine." And he said to them, "Go!" So they came out and entered the swine; and suddenly, the whole herd rushed down the steep bank into the sea and perished in the water. The swineherds ran off, and on going into the town, they told the whole story about what had happened to the demoniacs. Then the whole town came out to meet Jesus; and when they saw him, they begged him to leave their neighborhood. And after getting into a boat he crossed the sea and came to his own town. (Mt 8:18–9:1)

Photo by Lorna Patterson

Fig. 11 Fishing boat. On the Sea of Galilee visitors can sail across the water in a fishing boat modeled after an authentic first-century one discovered in the mud on the bottom of the lake.

Photo by Lorna Patterson

Fig. 12 View from the Mount of Beautitudes Church. The Mount of Beatitudes Church commands a view of the eastern shore, with the Golan Heights visible above it.

Jesus' Resurrection Appearance in Galilee

After these things Jesus showed himself again to the disciples by the Sea of Tiberias; and he showed himself in this way. Gathered there together were Simon Peter, Thomas called the Twin, Nathaniel of Cana in Galilee, the sons of Zebedee, and two others of his disciples. Simon Peter said to them, "I am going fishing." They said to him, "We will go with you." They went out and got into the boat, but that night they caught nothing.

Just after daybreak, Jesus stood on the beach; but the disciples did not know that it was Jesus. Jesus said to them, "Children, you have no fish, have you?" They answered him, "No." He said to them, "Cast the net to the right side of the boat, and you will find some." So they cast it, and now they were not able to haul it in because there were so many fish. That disciple whom Jesus loved said to Peter, "It is the Lord!" When Simon Peter heard that it was the Lord, he put on some clothes, for he was naked, and jumped into the sea. But the other disciples came in the boat, dragging the net full of fish, for they were not far from the land, only about a hundred yards off.

When they had gone ashore, they saw a charcoal fire there, with fish on it, and bread. Jesus said to them, "Bring some of the fish that you have just caught." So Simon Peter went aboard and hauled the net ashore, full of large fish, a hundred fifty-three of them; and though there were so many, the net was not torn. Jesus said to them, "Come and have breakfast." Now none of the disciples dared to ask him, "Who are you?" because they knew it was the Lord. Jesus came and took the bread and gave it to them, and did the same with the fish. This was now the third time that Jesus appeared to the disciples after he was raised from the dead.

When they had finished breakfast, Jesus said to Simon Peter, "Simon son of John, do you love me more than these?" He said to him, "Yes, Lord, you know that I love you." Jesus said to him, "Feed my lambs." A second time he said to him, "Simon son of John, do you love me?" He said to him, "Yes, Lord, you know that I love you." He said to him, "Tend my sheep." He said to him the third time, "Simon son of John, do you love me?" Peter felt hurt because he said to him the third time, "Do you love me?" And he said to him, "Lord, you know everything; you know that I love you." Jesus said to him, "Feed my sheep. Very truly, I tell you, when you were younger, you used to fasten your own belt and to go wherever

30

you wished. But when you grow old, you will stretch out your hands, and someone else will fasten a belt around you and take you where you do not wish to go." (He said this to indicate the kind of death by which he would glorify God.) After this he said to him, "Follow me." (Jn 21:1-19)

Photo by Lorna Patterson

Fig. 13 Statue of Jesus and Peter. On Galilee's western shore a statue depicts the site where tradition holds that Jesus gave the primacy to Peter as narrated in John's Gospel, "Feed my lambs....Feed my sheep" (Jn 21:15–17).

Photo by Lorna Patterson

Fig. 14 Sunrise over the water. Sunrise over the water illustrates another line from the same passage in John: "Just after daybreak, Jesus stood on the beach..." (Jn 21:4).

Notes

1. Nun, Mendel, "Ports of Galilee," *Biblical Archaeology Review* 25:4 (1999), 18–31. Names of the villages surrounding the Sea of Galilee were in part taken from the twenty-five-year research and exploration of this author.
2. Morton, H. V., *In the Steps of the Master*, New York: Dodd, Mead & Co. (1937). Few books can surpass Morton's graphic narrative descriptions of the Holy Land.
3. Arav, Remi, Freund, Richard A., and Shroder, John F. "Bethsaida Rediscovered," *Biblical Archaeology Review* 26:1 (2000), 44–56. Excavation of Bethsaida is ongoing, so the information used in my text based on the findings of these archaeologists may not be conclusive.
4. Nun, "Ports of Galilee," 18–21.
5. Wachsmann, Shelly, "The Galilee Boat—2000-Year-Old Hull Recovered Intact," *Biblical Archaeology Review* 14:5 (1988), 19–33. Dubbed "the Jesus boat" in Israeli papers, this exciting discovery was made near Capernaum in February 1988. This preserved fishing boat hull dates from the time of Christ.
6. Yeivin, Ze'ev, "Ancient Chorozain Comes Back to Life," *Biblical Archaeology Review* 13:5 (1987), 22–28. A comprehensive summary of the excavation at the site with useful photos and diagrams.
7. Gonen, Rivka, *Biblical Holy Places: An Illustrated Guide*, Israel: Palphot LTD (1987), pp. 183–84. Although a pilgrimage site since early Christianity, Magdala has not been developed for modern visitors as has Capernaum excavations began in 1973 and are ongoing.
8. Josephus, Flavius, Wars of the Jews, 3:516, *The Works of Josephus: New Updated Edition*, trans. William Whiston, Peabody, Maine: Hendrickson Publisher, Inc. (2000), p. 662.
9. Murphy-O'Connor, Jerome, O.P., *The Holy Land: An Oxford Archaeological Guide from Earliest Times to 1700*, 4th ed. New York: Oxford University Press (1998), p. 14.
10. Loffreda, S., O.F.M., *Recovering Capernaum*, Jerusalem: Franciscan Printing Press (1990). Loffreda, together with fellow excavator V. Corbo, O.F.M., has published extensive material on Capernaum. Some of their work (originally in Italian) has been translated into English.
11. Murphy-O'Connor, *Holy Land*, pp. 218–20. Both the synagogue and the church-house (or basilica) were built in Byzantine times (fourth century). Some hostility existed between the two communities, Jewish

and Christian, which may account for the building of Peter's church-house. "The Synagogue was erected in the Byzantine period and given the rivalry between the two communities it is not improbable that its construction (the Synagogue) inspired the transformation of the house-church."

12.   Loffreda, *Capernaum*, p. 63. "On paleographic grounds, the graffiti can be dated from the beginning of the third century to the early fifth century." According to Loffreda, the Christian character of the church-house is clearly vindicated: "In fact the name and the monogram of Jesus occur in several graffiti. Jesus is called the Lord, Christ, the Most High."

13.   Ibid., p. 63. Archaeologist Loffreda comments on the importance of Egeria's early testimony: "Nobody can miss the striking accuracy of Egeria's description in the light of our archaeological discoveries."

14.   Ibid., pp. 41–47.

15.   Burri, Rene, *H. V. Morton: In Search of the Holy Land*, New York: Dodd, Mead, and Co. (1979), p. 63. This extract from Morton's classic *In the Steps of the Master* is published with other extracts from the same book along with striking photographs by Rene Burri.

16.   Hoade, Eugene, O.F.M., *Guide to the Holy Land*, Jerusalem: Franciscan Press (1973), pp. 45–46.

Star in Nativity grotto marking the traditional birth place of Christ

Western retaining wall and Muslim Dome of the Rock in Jerusalem

Devout Jews praying at the Western Wall

Mass celebrated in the Church of the Holy Sepulcher on Mount Calvary

The Garden of Gethsemane on the Mount of Olives

Tomb of Jessus in the
Holy Sepulcher
Basilica in Jerusalem

Remains of Herod's seaport on the Mediterranean coast

Cave #4 by the Dead Sea, where some the Dead Sea Scrolls were found

Chapter 2
JERUSALEM

Photo by Lorna Patterson

Fig. 15 Old Jerusalem as seen today looking west from the Mount of Olives.

I was glad when they said to me,
    "Let us go to the house of the LORD!"
Our feet are standing
    within your gates, O Jerusalem.
Jerusalem—built as a city
    that is bound firmly together.
To it the tribes go up,
    the tribes of the LORD,
as was decreed for Israel,
    to give thanks to the name of the LORD.

For there the thrones for judgment were set up,
    the thrones of the house of David.
Pray for the peace of Jerusalem:
    "May they prosper who love you.
Peace be within your walls,
    and security within your towers."
For the sake of my relatives and friends
    I will say, "Peace be within you."
For the sake of the house of the LORD our God,
    I will seek your good. (Ps 122)

The Old Walled City Today

Standing on barren rocky heights, one sees in Jerusalem a totally different picture from the verdant rolling hills of Galilee. The Holy Land is full of startling contrasts; this is only one of them.

For a panoramic view of this unique city, one can walk the ramparts and circle the entire wall in about an hour. A glimpse below brings into focus the crowd-packed streets with their bustling shops and small courtyards. From time to time in the early morning a cock will add its noisy contribution to clamoring din. Israeli soldiers toting ominous M-16s mingle about in the surging throng.

From these fifty-foot-high battlements, the observer can look down upon all four traditional quarters: Muslim, Christian, Armenian, and Jewish. Each quarter has its own entrance gate as well as its own distinct flavor. Towering Jaffa Gate on the western side is the main entrance from modern Jerusalem, opening into the Armenian and Jewish areas. New Gate on the north side ushers one into the Christian Quarter. Most impressive of all, the Damascus Gate leads directly into the Muslim section. To really get the feel of old Jerusalem, one must stay within its ancient walls, wander its narrow winding streets, absorb its sounds—the Hebrew chanting at the Western Wall, the *muezzin's* call to prayer, the deep-throated church bells summoning the faithful.

To most of the world's population, Jerusalem is identified with the old walled city, this square mile within the medieval ramparts. What is seen today was actually built by Sultan Sulieman the Magnificent in the sixteenth century. However, for some visitors the first-time encounter with these walls is almost like a vision from the ancient past. Historically, this sacred city is the focal point of the world's three great monotheistic religions. Symbolically, the walls are a reminder of Jerusalem's violent past. Although the name *Jerusalem* means "city of peace," it has seen little of it during the past centuries. Tension, unrest, and violence mark the area.

Of course, over time Jerusalem has changed; indeed it has dramatically expanded in recent years, especially to the west, where it is much like any modern city. And the encroachment of Israelis upon hereditary Palestinian-owned land around the Old City is a subject of continual controversy and discord.

Reconstructing Jerusalem at the Time of Christ

All this is Jerusalem today. But how did it look in the time of Jesus? Over the ages much has been buried and lies beneath layers of broken rubble. To reconstruct the city as it was two thousand years ago is difficult if not impossible. An Israeli scholar, Professor Avi-Yonah, after long research, has created an impressive outdoor scale model (1:50) of Herodian Jerusalem on the grounds of the Holy Land Hotel in west Jerusalem. Based on sources such as the New Testament and the Talmud, historians such as Flavius Josephus, and modern archaeology, the model helps us visualize the city as it was in the time of Jesus. Not all details have the same value, but the Temple and Temple Mount are considered quite reliable.

Especially important in recent times has been the contribution of archaeology. A veritable explosion of archaeological excavation has taken place in the Old City since 1967. As excavation and research have progressed, some sites, even though hallowed by long tradition, wither under the scrutiny of archaeological discoveries. Such for example is the traditional Via Dolorosa or Way of the Cross, which both historians and archaeologists today reject as the authentic route taken by Jesus on the way to Calvary. Much depends on the identification of the *praetorium*, the location of the judgment hall where Jesus was condemned by Pilate. Most scholars, such as Frs. Benoit and Murphy-O'Connor, believe that evidence shows that the praetorium was at Herod's palace, which is the site of the present-day Citadel. If so, the

Map 4
THE OLD CITY OF JERUSALEM TODAY

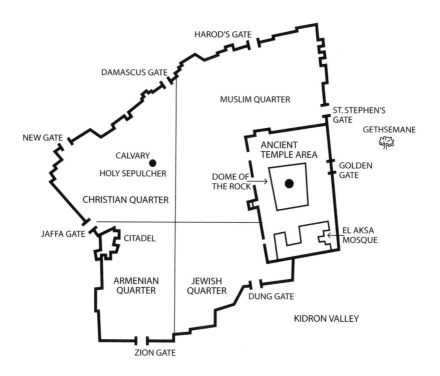

Way of the Cross would have begun there, not at the *lithostraton* (stone pavement) underneath the convent of the Sisters of Zion as once thought. With the advances of archaeology, many new reconstructions of the Old City have been made.[1]

Nevertheless, some places are certain beyond any reasonable doubt. Such, for example, are the Mount of Olives overlooking the Valley of Kidron and the Temple Mount where the Muslim Dome of the Rock now stands. Somewhere in this enclosed area was the magnificent temple Herod built and that Jesus knew so well. It is certain from the Gospels that Christ looked down from the Mount of Olives over the city he loved.

The Monumental Staircase

Although some traditional sites have been disproved by excavations and research of recent archaeology, others that were previously known only from ancient written sources such as Josephus in his Antiquities of the Jews have been confirmed. An example of special interest to Christians is the uncovering of the area around the southern end of the Temple Mount. Unearthed here are the monumental steps that pilgrims used at the time of Christ to enter the Temple.

"If I were a Christian," says Jerusalem archaeologist Prof. Dan Bahat, "I would build a shrine here. The likelihood that Mary, Joseph and Jesus climbed on these same steps is very strong" (Bahat lecture, *Casa Nova*, Jan 1988). From Josephus it is known that this monumental staircase was used by pilgrims entering the Temple area for special feasts such as the Passover. Among them would have been the Holy Family.

In all there are thirty steps carved out of the natural bedrock with a total width of 210 feet. Steps alternate with landings to ensure a slow and reverent approach to the Temple. At the top is a landing or platform from which Jewish teachers spoke to the crowds below. Jesus himself probably used this site for the same purpose. At the bottom of the stairway is a *mikveh* (ritual bath) with pools in which Jesus and his disciples would likely have immersed themselves according to Jewish rites of purification.[2]

Such is the kind of evidence archaeology has to offer, which may or may not be helpful to the first-time devout pilgrim to Jerusalem. Some visitors find it a comfort to know with some certitude that it is possible to walk on the same stones on which Christ trod some two thousand years ago. But most important is the theological meaning of the sites, not only these in particular but of Jerusalem as a whole. For this we need a guide; and none interprets the significance of Jerusalem more clearly than Luke, the author of the third Gospel. The theological meaning of Jerusalem is the dominating theme in Luke's account. Unlike the other Gospel writers,

Map 5
PLAN OF THE TEMPLE COMPLEX

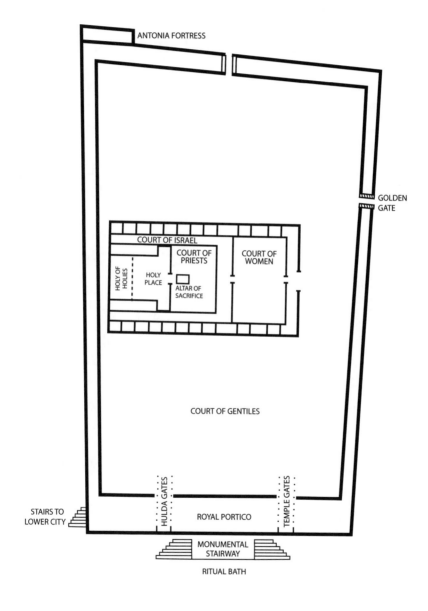

ANTONIA FORTRESS

GOLDEN GATE

COURT OF ISRAEL

COURT OF PRIESTS

COURT OF WOMEN

HOLY OF HOLIES

HOLY PLACE

ALTAR OF SACRIFICE

COURT OF GENTILES

STAIRS TO LOWER CITY

HULDA GATES

ROYAL PORTICO

TEMPLE GATES

MONUMENTAL STAIRWAY

RITUAL BATH

Luke makes no mention of events outside Jerusalem; for him every-thing begins and ends in the Holy City.

Jerusalem According to Luke

In reading Luke's Gospel one has the sense of traveling with Christ to the sacred city for the last time. Such phrases as "Jesus was going up to Jerusalem" or "as he was going along" include the reader as a companion on the journey. Events in the public ministry of Jesus are scattered throughout other Gospels; not so in Luke. Both literally and symbolically, this journey will be culminated in the sacrificial climax on Calvary, since here Jesus is to accomplish his mission, the redemption of mankind. As depicted by Luke, this journey is initiated in chapter 9 and is completed later, in chapter 19. Its beginning is more explicit and solemn than those of the other Gospels: "When the days drew near for him to be taken up, he set his face to go to Jerusalem. And he sent messengers ahead of him" (Lk 9:51–52).

In a certain sense, the hidden life of Christ can be incorporated into this journey to Jerusalem. For every year, at the time of the Pasch, even as a boy, Jesus went up to Jerusalem with his parents. The Holy Family faithfully followed Jewish custom. And their entrance into the Temple area would have been up the monumental staircase recently uncovered by archaeologists.

Just one instance of Jesus' boyhood trip to Jerusalem is given; it is found in Luke. Traveling some eighty miles from Nazareth to Jerusalem was quite a distance, especially when the trek was mostly on foot. Pilgrims generally traveled in groups with relatives or friends, moving together in little caravans that spent the nights in stopover areas. Upon reaching Jerusalem, pilgrims often stayed with relatives or friends, as Joseph, Mary, and Jesus probably did in the area on the Mount of Olives near Bethany. The city of Jerusalem would be jammed with teeming crowds on such festive occasions, making lodging a problem.

As a young boy, Jesus likely climbed those monumental steps entering the Temple area, helped along by Joseph. How children entered the Temple at the time of Christ depended on the age of the child and the school of thought one followed on the subject. According to some, entrance to the Temple was restricted to the child who could climb the Temple stairs if his father held his hand. Others contended that a son who could sit astride his father's shoulders should be brought to the Temple.

In any case, we know that Jesus made the Temple visit at the age of twelve. Once again Luke emphasizes the Temple's significance—a symbol of the reality that is Jesus himself. Of course his enemies did not understand, charging, "We heard him say, 'I will destroy this temple that is made with hands, and in three days I will build another, not made with hands'"(Mk 14:5–8).

When the young Jesus entered the Temple, his parents must have climbed the thirty steps one sees today at least twice in their effort to find their lost son. With great anxiety, Luke tells us, they returned to Jerusalem seeking the boy Jesus. Upon finding him surrounded by learned teachers in the Temple, his mother remonstrated, "'Child, why have you treated us like this? Look, your father and I been searching for you in great anxiety.' He said to them, '...Did you not know that I must be in my Father's house?' But they did not understand what he said to them. Then he went down with them to...Nazareth, and was obedient to them. His mother treasured all these things in her heart" (Lk 2:48–51).

The Mount of Olives: Dominus Flevit *and* Gethsemane

Later on in his narrative, Luke underscores the importance of Jerusalem when he portrays Jesus looking down upon the city from the Mount of Olives. Once again, it is Luke who catches the scene and its somber mood so vividly: "As he came near and saw the city, he wept over it, saying, 'If you, even you, had only recognized on this day the things that make for peace!...How often have I desired to gather your children together as a hen gathers her brood under her wings, and you were not willing!" (Lk 19:41; 13:34).

Of course, the exact site of this scene is not known—somewhere on the western side of the Mount of Olives overlooking the city. But Italian architect Antonio Barluzzi has erected a small chapel commemorating the event known as *Dominus Flevit* ("the Lord wept") built in the shape of a teardrop with the Temple Mount visible through the windowed wall above the altar.

Down a bit further is another architectural gem, Barluzzi's little church commemorating the agony of Christ in the Garden of Gethsemane. Traditionally, here is where Jesus prayed, "Father, if you are willing, remove this cup from me; yet not my will but yours be done" (Lk 22:42). Once again, Barluzzi has captured the sorrowful atmosphere heightened by muted violet shadows filtering through purple glass windows.

No one knows the exact spot where Jesus prayed during his agony; but since the area is near the ancient road leading from the Temple to the summit of the Mount of Olives it is considered most likely. Over the site is a chapel called the Church of All Nations beside a garden and ancient olive trees. After celebrating the Passover with the twelve (Judas having left to betray him), Jesus descended from the Cenacle on the western hill in the Upper City, passed by the pool of

Siloam in the Kidron Valley on his way to the Garden of Gethsemane (Mk 14:26, 32).

Actually the Mount of Olives is a ridge sloping up from the barren Kidron. In any other place it would seem arid and inhospitable; but in contrast to Jerusalem it was then (as it is today) a haven of peace, a place to go and escape the tensions of the city. In such a place Jesus was arrested, already knowing he would be betrayed. This was a moment of decision. In a matter of minutes he could have walked up to the summit of the Mount of Olives, then gone out of the city into the desert. The decision was clear. His choice was made.

Map 6
PRINCIPAL SITES OF CHRIST'S PASSION

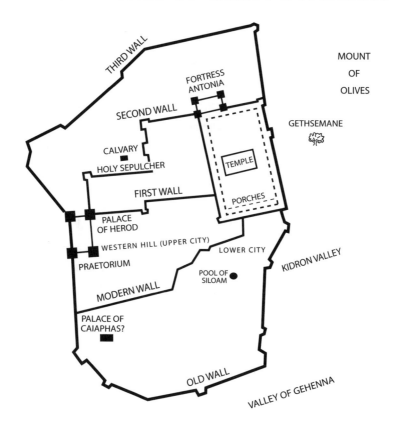

The Praetorium and Lithostraton: Authenticity Issues

After his arrest, and after confrontation with the high priest Caiphas and a night in prison, Jesus was led to the praetorium, the judgment hall of Pilate, from whence he would be made to carry his cross to Calvary. The praetorium was the residence of the provincial governor where Pilate stayed when he was in Jerusalem. There have been two generally accepted sites of the praetorium: one is the modern Citadel near the Jaffa Gate where Herod's palace was located in the time of Jesus; the other is the Fortress Antonia adjacent to the northwest corner of the Temple area. Here is a lithostraton or stone pavement that Saint John (19:3) refers to as the praetorium. Could this possibly be where Christ was judged before Pilate?

Covering the site today is the convent of the Sisters of Zion. Underneath their building was discovered a magnificent pavement near which was an arch where Pilate was thought to have said, "Behold the Man" (Latin: *Ecce homo*). But it is now certain that this is not the lithostraton mentioned in John's Gospel. The reasons for this are given by the noted Dominican theologian-archaeologist, Pere Benoit, O.P.[3]

According to Benoit, the praetorium or site where the condemnation of Jesus took place was at what today is called the Citadel—in the time of Christ, the area of Herod's palace. Jerome Murphy-O'Connor agrees, stating flatly that the condemnation of Jesus took place at the Citadel. If this be true, then the Via Dolorosa or Way of the Cross did not begin near the Fortress Antonia, as held by medieval tradition, but rather from the area of the Citadel, whose exact route is still unknown.[4]

Should this new knowledge dampen the devotion of pilgrims who still make the stations of the cross along the same route every Friday? It must be said that the archaeological facts and historical accuracy are one thing; but religious devotion is entirely something else. As Murphy-O'Connor has expressed it, the "Via Dolorosa is defined by faith, not by history."[5] Perhaps the best explanation is that of Sister Brigett Martin-Chave, who lives at the Sisters of Zion Convent. She says that people have attached religious meaning to archaeological remains that should not be and adds, "I want to put things in their real light. People need help in visualizing the way things happened. And that is fine. But this is not the place where they really happened. Through pilgrimages the convent acquired a sanctity that history may not have bestowed upon it. This site has been made holy by the prayers that have been offered here over the years."[6]

What applies to the convent of the Sisters of Zion may also be relevant to another "deposed biblical site"—the Garden Tomb mistakenly thought by some to be the burial site of Christ. This site stands not far from Damascus Gate in North Jerusalem, near the École Biblique of the Dominican Fathers. The so-called Garden Tomb was the dream-child of famous British general Charles Gordon, the hero of Khartoum in the nineteenth century. Certainly the location is more beautiful than the Holy Sepulcher, but the tomb here has been deemed inauthentic because it lacks solid historical and archaeological evidence.[7]

Even though such spots have their function as helpful visual aids, they ought not to be confused with the real thing. However, an undeniable value of the Garden Tomb is that it can enable one to envision how the site of Christ's burial might have looked before being covered over with two thousand years of history. Quiet and peaceful (unlike the scene at the Holy Sepulcher), this lovely spot can enable one to contemplate the events of Christ's passion and death. As Pere Pierre Benoit remarked in an interview at the École Biblique in Jerusalem, "Faith does not depend on the details of history."[8]

The Holy Sepulcher, Calvary, and the Tomb

Inside the walls of the Old City are the Holy Sepulcher and Calvary, both under the same roof of an enormous rambling basilica that is essentially the same edifice left in the twelfth century by the Crusaders. Badly in need of repair, the building can be a disappointment to many Christians. In recent years, some progress toward restoration has been made.

According to the New Testament, Christ suffered crucifixion on a skull-shaped knoll outside the city walls. But since the first century, the site has been enclosed inside the walls of the Old City. Most archaeologists agree that, beyond any reasonable doubt, all evidence points to the area occupied by the Holy Sepulcher as the authentic site of Calvary and the Tomb.

In the 1960s, well-known British archaeologist Kathleen Kenyon discovered evidence of a rock quarry and first-century Jewish tombs where the Holy Sepulcher is today. In fact, visitors can see two of these tombs immediately behind the burial place revered as that of Jesus himself. Such evidence is proof that the area was outside the walls of the city at the time of Christ, because Jewish law forbade burials within the city itself.

Still, Christianity's most sacred site does not look like what one might expect from reading the Gospels. One would think that the holiest of all Christian spots ought to be found in splendid isolation, a quiet fitting place for prayer and contemplation. Instead, the pilgrim or visitor is often confronted by what appears to be a religious mob scene, complete with a cacophony of chants, processions, and liturgies involving Greek Orthodox, Armenians, Roman Catholics, and Copts.

Enormous and somewhat confusing, the Holy Sepulcher today essentially is the same structure the Crusaders left behind after conquering Jerusalem in 1099. The fourth-century church of Constantine has been reconstructed almost out of existence, leaving us little evidence of its original appearance. A deeper knowledge of the building's long history is a key element in appreciating this holiest site in Christendom.

History of the Holy Sepulcher: Authenticity

That early Jewish Christians were interested in the place where Jesus died and was buried is certainly understandable. Indeed, some were eyewitnesses to his death and burial. Others were early converts, as narrated in the Acts of the Apostles. From the beginning. Jewish Christians came to reverence the site. To discourage this practice, the Roman emperor Hadrian ordered that Calvary and the Tomb be completely covered by an earth-filled terrace. A statue of Jupiter was erected above Calvary, and an altar dedicated to Venus over the Tomb. Contrary to Hadrian's intent, this only served to mark with certitude the exact spot. In 326, Constantine the Great had the temples pulled down and the terrace completely removed. Much to his surprise and that of Christians, both Calvary and the Tomb were still intact. They had simply been covered over. Eusebuis of Caesarea, an eyewitness and first church historian, left the following account: "At once the work was carried out, and as layer after layer of the subsoil came into view, the venerable and most holy memorial of the Savior's resurrection beyond all our hopes came into view."[9]

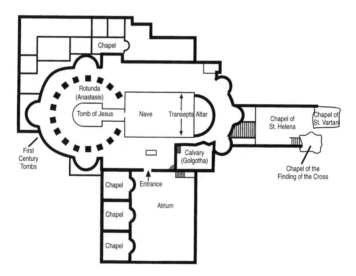

Fig. 16 The Crusader Holy Sepulcher Church. The form of the church that one sees today dates back to the twelfth century. The Tomb of Jesus enclosed by the rotunda called *Anastasis* ("resurrection") is the focal point. Golgotha (right side of diagram) on the upper level is divided into two chapels: the "Latin Calvary" and the "Greek Calvary." The chapels of St. Helena, St. Vartan, and the Finding of the Cross are located on the lower subterranean level. Remains of an ancient quarry are still evident in St. Vartan's chapel.

On this exact location Constantine began to build his mammoth church, which was dedicated in A.D. 335. An enormous structure, the building was much larger than the church one sees today. At the time it was considered a wonder of the ancient world. Four rows of columns divided the church into five naves 150 feet long and eighty-five feet wide. The Tomb was covered by a circular edifice called the *Anastasis* (Resurrection) and all the rock around it removed. According to ancient reports, Constantine's original basilica was a magnificent sight, a building constructed by the best craftsmen in Western Europe. Calvary was only a few yards away; but it was not covered under the same roof with the Tomb until the time of Crusaders in the twelfth century.[10]

Constantine's church continued to be used until the Persians destroyed it in A.D. 614. Restored, though poorly, it remained until attacked again by the fanatical Egyptian Caliph Hakim, who systematically hacked the Tomb to pieces. Truly, it was so completely pulverized with axes and iron bars that nothing remained. Only the rotunda was left, which the Crusaders rebuilt into the form one sees today. Almost destroyed by fire in 1808, the shrine was rebuilt again, this time by the Greeks. Unfortunately they took the opportunity to destroy everything Latin and Western, including valuable works of art and tombs of the Western Crusader knights.[11]

In 1927, a serious earthquake so weakened the basilica that British engineers were called in to erect huge supporting beams to keep the edifice from falling apart. Thus propped up, it remained standing until the 1950s, when a more ecumenical atmosphere prevailed. Since then, the Greeks, Armenians, and Catholics have been able to cooperate in trying to restore the ancient structure to some of its original splendor. The most recent work completed just a short time ago was the gigantic and now very beautiful cupola.

Responsible for the care and upkeep of the Holy Sepulcher are the three ancient religious groups: the Armenians, the Greeks, and the Latins (Roman Catholics). A joint restoration project was begun in

1960 that also included extensive archaeological work designed to authenticate the history of one of the most complex and fascinating buildings in the world.

Thirteen trenches were excavated, not only to examine the stability of the Crusader structure, but also to enable archaeologists to probe into the multilayered history of the site. Walls were opened up to reveal earlier structures, and a modern drainage system was installed. Soundings were made for purely archaeological purposes. According to Dan Bahat, the results of all this investigation and research confirmed the established tradition that this is indeed the site always believed to be Calvary and the Holy Sepulcher.[12]

"The results of all this research," says the Israeli archaeologist, "have now been published in a three-volume final report by Virgil C. Corbo, O.F.M., professor of archaeology at the Studium Franciscanum of Jerusalem. Father Corbo has been deeply involved in this archaeological work for more than twenty years, and no one is better able to report on the results than he."[13]

Originally the site was a rock quarry, as can be seen from the limestone chiseled out in square blocks for building purposes. The quarry, as deep as forty feet in some places, was filled with earth, ash, and pottery dating as far back as Iron Age II. "In the first century A.D. the quarry was converted into a garden and orchard...and at the same time [it] also became a cemetery. At least four tombs dating from this period have been found."[14]

Another type of tomb called *arcosolium* was also common to this period. "The so-called tomb of Jesus...is composed of an antechamber and a rock-hewn arcosolium. Unfortunately centuries of pilgrims have completely deformed this tomb by pecking and chipping away bits of rock as souvenirs or for their reliquaries. Today the tomb is completely covered with later masonry; but enough is known to date it from about the turn of the era."[15]

Jerusalem:
Its Universal Significance

Jerusalem! No city has meant so much, for so many, for so long a time. No city in the world has evoked such emotion, passion, and even violence. For centuries people have loved it, revered it, fought for it, died for it. It is no different now. From the Mount of Olives Jesus wept over it; he warned of its future destruction, foretelling, "When you see Jerusalem surrounded by armies, then know that its desolation has come near" (Lk 21:20). Today, tension still holds sway as Palestinians and Israelis struggle over possession of this Holy City. As in past ages, modern pilgrims stand before its gates praying the ancient psalm, "Our feet are standing within your gates, O Jerusalem....'May they prosper who love you. Peace be within your walls, and security within your towers'" (Ps 122). But peace will only come with justice. As the psalmist goes on, "Love and faithfulness will meet; righteousness and peace will kiss" (Ps 85:10). The cycle of violence continues to wound this sacred land and its people because love and truth, justice and peace still seem to be so far from becoming a reality.

The Circumcision of Jesus

After eight days had passed, it was time to circumcise the child; and he was called Jesus, the name given by the angel before he was conceived in the womb. When the time came for their purification according to the law of Moses, they brought him up to Jerusalem to present him to the Lord (as it is written in the law of the Lord, "Every firstborn male shall be designated as holy to the Lord"), and they offered a sacrifice according to what is stated in the law of the Lord, "a pair of turtle doves or two young pigeons."

Now there was a man in Jerusalem whose name was Simeon; this man was righteous and devout, looking forward to the consolation of Israel, and the Holy Spirit rested on him. It had been revealed to him by the Holy Spirit that he would not see death before he had seen the Lord's Messiah. Guided by the Spirit, Simeon came into the temple; and when the parents brought in the child Jesus, to do for him what was customary under the law, Simeon took him in his arms and praised God, saying,

"Master, now you are dismissing
       your servant in peace,
    according to your word;
for my eyes have seen your salvation,
    which you have prepared in the
       presence of all peoples,
a light for revelation to the Gentiles
    and for the glory to your people Israel."

And the child's father and mother were amazed at what was being said about him. Then Simeon blessed them and said to his mother Mary, "This child is destined for the falling and rising of many in Israel, and to be a sign that will be opposed so that the inner thoughts of many will be revealed—and a sword will pierce your own soul too." (Luke 2:21–35)

Photo by Lorna Patterson

Fig. 17 Scale model of Temple. When Mary and Joseph brought the child Jesus to be circumcised, the Temple may have looked like this scale model of Avi-Yonah based on ancient sources. In the center is the tall Holy Place around which are courtyards: the Courts of the Gentiles, the Women, the Israelites, and the Priests.

Photo by Lorna Patterson

Fig. 18 Model of Temple showing the fortress Antonia and Calvary. Looking from west to east is the Temple with the fortress Antonia on the left (with four towers) and Calvary, the small white hill outside the wall in the center.

The Finding in the Temple

Now every year his parents went to Jerusalem for the festival of the Passover. And when he was twelve years old, they went up as usual for the festival. When the festival was ended and they started to return, the boy Jesus stayed behind in Jerusalem, but his parents did not know it. Assuming that he was in the group of travelers, they went a day's journey. Then they started to look for him among their relatives and friends. When they did not find him, they returned to Jerusalem to search for him. After three days they found him in the temple, sitting among the teachers, listening to them and asking them questions. And all who heard him were amazed at his understanding and his answers. When his parents saw him they were astonished; and his mother said to him, "Child, why have you treated us like this? Look, your father and I have been searching for you in great anxiety." He said to them, "Why were you searching for me? Did you not know that I must be in my Father's house?" But they did not understand what he said to them. Then he went down with them and came to Nazareth, and was obedient to them. And his mother treasured all these things in her heart.

And Jesus increased in wisdom and in years, and in divine and human favor. (Lk 2:41–52)

Photo by Lorna Patterson

Fig. 19 Temple stairs. Since 1967, archaeological excavations have uncovered the broad monumental stairway leading up to what was the Temple area in Herodian times. At the time of Christ this was the entrance to the Temple area used by pilgrims coming to the feast of the Passover. Above the stairway was the Royal Portico bordering the Court of the Gentiles. The steps were carved into the natural bedrock, so hardly any restoration was needed after their discovery.

The Agony in the Garden

Then Jesus went with them to a place called Gethsemane; and he said to his disciples, "Sit here while I go over there and pray." He took with him Peter and the two sons of Zebedee, and began to be grieved and agitated. Then he said to them, "I am deeply grieved, even to death; remain here and stay awake with me." And going a little farther, he threw himself on the ground and prayed, "My Father, if it be possible, let this cup pass from me; yet not what I want but what you want." Then he came to the disciples and found them sleeping; and he said to Peter, "So, could you not stay awake with me one hour? Stay awake and pray that you may not come into the time of trial; the spirit indeed is willing, but the flesh is weak." Again he went away for the second time and prayed, "My Father, if this cannot pass unless I drink it, your will be done." Again he came and found them sleeping, for their eyes were heavy. So leaving them again, he went away and prayed for the third time, saying the same words. Then he came to the disciples and said to them, "Are you still sleeping and taking your rest? See the hour is at hand, and the Son of Man is betrayed into the hands of sinners. Get up, let us be going. See, my betrayer is at hand." (Mt 26:36–46)

Jesus Is Arrested

While he was still speaking, Judas, one of the twelve, arrived; with him was a large crowd with swords and clubs, from the chief priests and the elders of the people. Now the betrayer had given them a sign, saying, "The one I will kiss is the man; arrest him." At once he came up to Jesus and said, "Greetings, Rabbi!" and kissed him. Jesus said to him, "Friend, do what you are here to do." And they came and laid hands on Jesus and arrested him. Suddenly, one of those with Jesus put his hand on his sword, drew it, and struck the slave of the high priest, cutting off his ear. Then Jesus said to him, "Put your sword back into its place; for all who take the sword will perish by the sword. Do you thing that I cannot appeal to my Father, and he will at once send me more than twelve legions of angels? But how then would the scriptures be fulfilled, which say it must happen in this way?" At that hour Jesus said to the crowds, "Have you come out with swords and clubs to arrest me as though I were a bandit? Day after day I sat in the temple teaching, and you did not arrest me. But all this has taken place, so that the scriptures of the prophets may be fulfilled." Then all the disciples deserted him and fled. (Mt 26:47–56)

Photo by Tom Patterson

Fig. 20 Garden of Gethsemane. The Garden of Gethsemane on the Mount of Olives still has several ancient olive trees. The University of California applied carbon-dating tests that indicated that some of the roots and wood may be more than two thousand years old.

Photo by Tom Patterson

Fig. 21 Church of the Agony. Near the olive grove is the Church of the Agony built over the traditional site where Jesus prayed. Of course, no one can be certain of the exact spot where this occurred, but we are sure that the location of the garden is on the Mount of Olives. Within the church, before the altar, is preserved an area of bedrock thought to be the place where Jesus petitioned his Father to "remove this cup from me" (Lk 22:42).

Jesus Is Crucified on Calvary

As they went out, they came upon a man from Cyrene named Simon; they compelled this man to carry his cross. And when they came to a place called Golgotha (which means Place of a Skull), they offered him wine to drink, mixed with gall; but when he tasted it, he would not drink it. And when they had crucified him, they divided his clothes among themselves by casting lots; then they sat down there and kept watch over him. Over his head they put the charge against him, which read, "This is Jesus, the King of the Jews."

Then two bandits were crucified with him, one on his right and one on his left. Those who passed by derided him, shaking their heads and saying, "You who would destroy the temple and build it in three days, save yourself! If you are the Son of God, come down from the cross." In the same way the chief priests also, along with the scribes and elders, were mocking him, saying, "He saved others; himself he cannot save. He is the King of Israel; let him come down from the cross now, and we will believe in him. He trusts in God; let God deliver him now, if he wants to; for he said, 'I am God's Son.'" The bandits who were crucified with him also taunted him in the same way.

From noon on, darkness came over the whole land until three in the afternoon. And about three o'clock Jesus cried with a loud voice, *"Eli, Eli, lema sabachthani?"* that is, "My God, my God, why have you forsaken me?" When some of the bystanders heard it, they said, "This man is calling for Elijah." At once one of them ran and got a sponge, filled it with sour wine, put it on a stick, and gave it to him to drink. But the others said, "Wait, let us see whether Elijah will come to save him." And then Jesus cried again with a loud voice and breathed his last. At that moment the curtain of the temple was torn in two, from top to bottom. The earth shook, and the rocks were split. The tombs also were opened, and many bodies of the saints who had fallen asleep were raised. After his resurrection they came out of the tombs and entered the holy city and appeared to many. Now when the centurion and those with him, who were keeping watch over Jesus, saw the earthquake and what took place, they were terrified and said, "Truly this man was God's Son!" (Mt 27:32–54)

Photo by Lorna Patterson

Fig. 22 Holy Sepulcher Church. Past the entrance to the Holy Sepulcher, immediately on the right, nineteen steep stone steps ascend to Calvary, where there are two chapels. This floor is on a level with the top of the skull-shaped hill called Golgotha on which Christ was crucified. On the right is the Roman Catholic chapel shown below. On the left is the Greek Orthodox chapel (barely visible here), where some of the natural rock can be seen.

Photo by Lorna Patterson

Fig. 23 Interior of Roman Catholic chapel at Holy Sepulcher.

The Resurrection of Jesus

Early on the first day of the week, while it was still dark, Mary Magdalene came to the tomb and saw that the stone had been removed from the tomb. So she ran and went to Simon Peter and the other disciple, the one whom Jesus loved, and said to them, "They have taken the Lord out of the tomb, and we do not know where they have laid him." Then Peter and the other disciple set out and went toward the tomb. The two were running together, but the other disciple outran Peter and reached the tomb first. He bent down to look in and saw the linen wrappings lying there, but he did not go in. Then Simon Peter came, following him, and went into the tomb. He saw the linen wrappings lying there, and the cloth that had been on Jesus' head, not lying with the linen wrappings but rolled up in a place by itself. Then the other disciple, who reached the tomb first, also went in, and he saw and believed; for as yet they did not understand the scripture, that he must rise from the dead. Then the disciples returned to their homes.

But Mary stood weeping outside the tomb. As she wept, she bent over to look into the tomb, and she saw two angels in white, sitting where the body of Jesus had been lying, one at the head and the other at the feet. They said to her, "Woman, why are you weeping?" She said to them, "They have taken away my Lord, and I do not know where they have laid him." When she had said this, she turned around and saw Jesus standing there, but she did not know that it was Jesus. Jesus said to her, "Woman, why are you weeping? Whom are you looking for?" Supposing him to be the gardener, she said to him, "Sir, if you have carried him away, tell me where you have laid him, and I will take him away." Jesus said to her, "Mary!" She turned and said to him in Hebrew, *"Rabbouni!"* (which means Teacher). Jesus said to her, "Do not hold on to me, because I have not yet ascended to the Father. But go to my brothers and say to them, 'I am ascending to my Father and your Father, to my God and your God!'" (Jn 20:1–17)

Fig. 24 Location of Jesus' tomb. Although reconstructed over the centuries, the location of the tomb where Jesus was buried is beyond any reasonable doubt. All scientific evidence available, besides an unbroken tradition of two thousand years, points to this one spot. As such it has been venerated by millions of believers down through the ages.

Photo by Lorna Patterson

Photo by Lorna Patterson

Fig. 25 First-century Jewish tombs. Near the tomb of Jesus, archaeologists have found other first-century Jewish tombs, indicating that this area indeed was used as a cemetery. This was in accordance with Jewish law that forbade burial inside the walls.

Photo by Lorna Patterson

Fig. 26 Dome of the Rock. Above the Western (Wailing) Wall appears the golden Dome of the Rock, where according to Muslim tradition Mohammed ascended to heaven. This mount is the likely site of the Jewish Temple at the time of Christ.

Photo by Lorna Patterson

Fig. 27 Praying at the Western Wall. Devout Jews pray at the wall day and night. The wall is not part of the Temple itself but a retaining wall built by Herod to enlarge the area upon which the edifice was built. On the left side of this photo is an archway close to the tunnel entrance recently extended along the Western Wall and emptying into the Muslim Quarter.

Notes

1. Ritmeyer, Kathleen, and Ritmeyer, Leen, "Reconstructing Herod's Temple Mount in Jerusalem," *Biblical Archaeology Review* 15:6 (1989), 23–42. This excellent article includes outstanding drawings of structures on the Temple Mount based on current archaeological evidence and ancient biblical and non-biblical writers.

2. Ibid., 36. Most of the monumental staircase is original with little reconstruction. Pilgrims entered the Temple area by climbing these steps.

3. Shanks, Hershel, "The Religious Message of the Bible: BAR Interviews Pere Benoit," *Biblical Archaeology Review* 12:2 (1986), 65. In an interview with Hershel Shanks, editor of *Biblical Archaeology Review*, Pere Benoit says that the pavement in the Sisters of Zion convent is beautiful but cannot be the one referred to in John 19:13 as the place where Jesus was judged before Pilate. "This pavement is built above a large cistern called The Struthion Pool. From Josephus we know that the pool was still not covered at the time of Titus' siege of Jerusalem in 70 A.D. It was open to the sky. The present pavement is built above the pool. It seals the pool. But in Jesus' time (c 30 A.D.) the pool was an open-air pool like the Bethesda pool. So there was no pavement here in Jesus time."

4 Murphy-O'Connor, Jerome, O.P., *The Holy Land: An Archaeological Guide*, New York: Oxford University Press (1998), p. 34.

5. Ibid., p. 35.

6. Shanks, "Religious Message of the Bible," 66.

7. Barkay, Gabriel, and Kloner, Amos, "The Garden Tomb: Was Jesus Buried Here?" *Biblical Archaeology Review* 12:2 (1986), 50. "There was never any sound scientific basis for locating the tomb of Jesus in the area of the Garden Tomb. The identification of the Garden Tomb as the tomb of Jesus thus reflects the psychology and atmosphere of the late 19th century Jerusalem rather than any new evidence—scientific, textual or archaeological."

8. Shanks, "Religious Message of the Bible," 58.

9. Murphy-O'Connor, *Holy Land*, p. 47. The author takes his quote from Eusebius's Life of Constantine (3:28). Eusebius, bishop of Caesarea in the fourth century A.D., was not only the first church historian but also an eyewitness of the uncovering of the location where Constantine built the Holy Sepulcher. His testimony along with the early Christian

community was of special value in supporting Constantine's decision to build the Holy Sepulcher on this particular spot.

10. Gonen, Rivka, *Biblical Holy Places: An Illustrated Guide,* Israel: Palphot LTD (1987), p. 131.

11. Hoade, Eugene, O.F.M., *Guide to the Holy Land,* Jerusalem: Franciscan Printing Press (1973), p. 105. These remarks of Hoade, though true, seem to reflect the hostility over conflicting rights in the Holy Sepulcher that existed for a long while between the Catholics and Greek Orthodox. Fortunately, a more ecumenical atmosphere now prevails.

12. See Dan Bahat's excellent article covering the project: "Does the Holy Sepulcher Church Mark the Burial of Jesus?" *Biblical Archaeology Review* 12:3 (1986), 26–45. The author is a distinguished Israeli archaeologist who also directed excavation of the controversial tunnel extending northward from the Western ("Wailing") Wall.

13. Ibid., 28.

14. Ibid., 30. Two of these four tombs mentioned by Bahat can be seen behind the Tomb of Jesus. Typical of these first-century tombs are the long recesses or *kokhim* in which a body could be placed. Two most easily seen are traditionally related to Nicodemus and Joseph of Arimathea (Jn 19:38–41, Lk 23:50–53; Mt 27:57–61).

15. Ibid., 30, 32.

Chapter 3
BETHLEHEM, NAZARETH, AND MOUNT TABOR

Sketch by Webster Patterson

Fig. 28 Basilica of Annunciation, Nazareth.

Map 7
PALESTINE: THE SOUTH

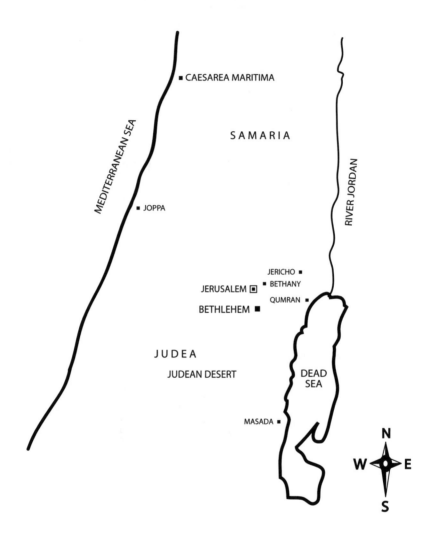

MEDITERRANEAN SEA

■ CAESAREA MARITIMA

SAMARIA

RIVER JORDAN

■ JOPPA

JERICHO ■
■ BETHANY
JERUSALEM ▣
QUMRAN ■
BETHLEHEM ■

JUDEA

JUDEAN DESERT

DEAD
SEA

MASADA ■

N
W ◆ E
S

Little is known about what are generally referred to as the "hidden years" of Jesus, which include his birth, his early childhood—indeed his first thirty years. What little we do know from the Gospels are the rather sketchy narratives of Matthew and Luke. Nevertheless, exploring the sacred sites of Bethlehem and Nazareth is an essential part of being a Christian because it emphasizes the humanity of Jesus, who was born and developed as we all do. These sites, as no others, eloquently say that he truly entered the human race—that he became one of us. Mount Tabor was included here because of its geographic proximity to Nazareth. The young Jesus would have been able to view it often and recall its place in Jewish history. Bethlehem, too, figures into his own ancestry, as the story of Ruth illustrates.

Ruth: The House of David Begins in Bethlehem

Bethlehem is about five miles south of Jerusalem. On a hilltop at the edge of the Judean Desert, the town is still surrounded by fields of barley, as it was in Old Testament times. It was in these fields that the story of Ruth begins. After the death of her husband in Moab, Ruth determined to follow her mother-in-law, Naomi, back to the older woman's homeland, Bethlehem. Finally giving in to her daughter-in-law's supplication, Naomi set out with Ruth on the long arduous journey to Judea. Upon arrival the two were so destitute that Ruth began to glean barley on a nearby farm. The land was owned by a kinsman named Boaz, who befriended Ruth. Through a series of creative maneuvers Ruth and Boaz fell in love, married, and eventually became the parents of Obed. Obed's son in turn was the father of Jesse, who was the father of David. And thus the lineage of Jesus began.

Such Old Testament stories flood one's consciousness as one enters Bethlehem today. The countryside that wraps itself around the town is still much the same. Sheaves of grain lie stacked beside the road; saffron stalks glisten in the sun. In this setting, it is not hard to envision Naomi and her devoted daughter-in-law, Ruth, and hear the latter saying, "Where you go, I will go; where you lodge, I will lodge; your people shall be my people, and your God my God" (Ruth 1:16).

Such are the biblical images Bethlehem evokes for the modern visitor. As one rounds a bend, it appears—"the little town of Bethlehem," as the carol goes, not so little as in ancient times but still tiny by modern standards. But there ends the Christmas-card image one has cherished from childhood. The town today does not look like the picture created by the Christmas crib and Saint Francis.

As might be expected, the ravages of time have taken their toll. However, two historical facts remain the same. Here, David, the future king of Israel, was born; and after him, the messiah. Neither fact has ever been seriously challenged. Perhaps nothing underlines this more than the layout of the town itself. Manger Square, with its Basilica of the Nativity, is the heart and soul of Bethlehem even today. Visitors and pilgrims continually streaming through make this the most visited site in modern Israel.[1]

The Church of the Nativity: History and Authenticity

The Basilica of the Nativity is built over the grotto where tradition holds that Jesus was born. The Gospels do not say that he was born in a cave; only that Mary wrapped the newborn child in swaddling clothes and laid him in a manger. But even now some houses in Bethlehem and its surroundings are still built in front of caves that serve as additional rooms, sometimes for use of animals. In the circumstances of Jesus' birth, the cave signaled a desire for privacy more than it did poverty.

The Church of the Nativity is the oldest continuously used Christian church in the world. As such, it has an interesting history. It was first built by Emperor Constantine in A.D. 339 and was enlarged by Byzantine emperor Justinian in the sixth century. In the seventh century, when Persians destroyed all Christian sites in the Holy Land, they paused when coming to this basilica, for there on the facade was a mosaic showing the wise men offering gifts to the Christ child. Since the magi were clothed in Persian garb, the warriors spared this one Christian shrine. The structure was renovated again by the Crusaders in the Middle Ages. What the visitor encounters today is the church left behind by the Crusaders, including the partially walled-up front entrance that requires one to bend low upon entering. Originally this was not out of reverence, but to prevent horsemen bent upon destruction from riding directly into the church.

Church of the Nativity: The Cave

Early Christians reverenced this cave-site from the beginning of the first century. To discourage this veneration, Emperor Hadrian had a pagan temple built over the place to try to erase all memory of Christ's birth. However, this served only to mark the location exactly. So when Constantine (A.D. 325) decided to build his basilica he had only to pull down Hadrian's temple and construct his church on the spot, conveniently but unknowingly preserved by the earlier pagan emperor.

Upon entering the basilica the visitor is confronted by a long nave with rows of ancient columns flanking its length. At the far end is the main high altar with stairs on each side leading down to the grotto below. The cave itself is fairly small, nineteen feet long and ten feet high, dimly lit with soft glowing candles that over the centuries have left their dark smudged contribution on the cave walls. On one side of the grotto one sees a fourteen-pointed silver star in a niche with the Latin inscription: *Hic de Virgine Maria Jesus Christus Natus Est* ("Here Jesus Christ was born of the Virgin Mary"). This is the actual place where Christ was born—where God became incarnate—as reverenced by Christians the world over for two thousand years.[2] Hushed silence pervades the area as pilgrims and visitors come and go. Breaking

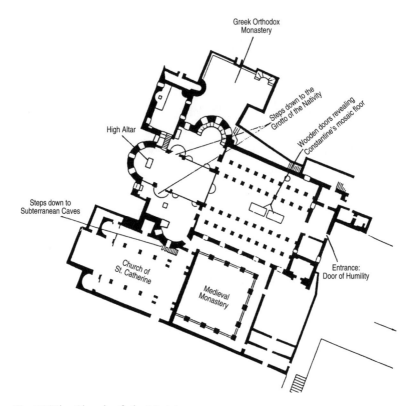

Fig. 29 The Church of the Nativity.

the silence from time to time, a group might sing a Christmas hymn such as "Silent Night" or pray aloud together in this universally revered holy place. At other times some may simply call out the names of beloved children, living or dead. Although the site does not conform to the Christmas crèche popularized in the thirteenth century, the visit for many is obviously a deeply moving religious experience. Despite the conflict between cherished childhood images and the reality, those present seem to sense that this is indeed a sacred site.

The Wise Men Appear: Theological Significance

Discussion of the Nativity is not complete without mention of the coming of the wise men found only in the Gospel of Matthew: "In the time of King Herod, after Jesus was born in Bethlehem of Judea, wise men from the East came to Jerusalem, asking 'Where is the child who has been born king of the Jews?'" (Mt 2:1–2). If this passage were found in Luke, we might suspect that the author introduced it to show fulfillment of Simeon's prophecy regarding Jesus as the "revelation to the Gentiles," since Luke himself was a Gentile. But since the account of the wise men is found only in Matthew, the most "Jewish" of the Gospels, there is nothing else to do but accept the facts as they are presented.

Questions about historical details in the infancy narratives are not easily answered, but one principle can be kept in mind: The scenes presented in these accounts are never merely historical. Both Gospel writers draw upon early Christian traditions in their infancy accounts, but each adapts them to a different theological purpose or meaning. Matthew emphasizes fulfillment of Old Testament prophecies; Luke stresses the free action of God involved in the birth of Jesus. For both the theological meaning is of primary importance, even though the emphasis is different in each case. Although one may not be able to verify every detail as historical, the theological meaning comes through.[3]

Even though this theological view is the most important consideration, many are fascinated by the colorful story of wise men coming from the East—an indefinite exotic location. Most favor Persia as the place and the magi followers of Zoroaster, perhaps astrologers. Matthew does not tell us how many wise men came; popular tradition has set the number anywhere from two to twelve. A mural on the wall in the catacomb of Domitilla shows four, two on each side of the Holy Family, probably for artistic balance. Most likely the number three is suggested by the three gifts that they offered.[4]

As scriptural scholar Raymond Brown has pointed out, the first part of chapter 2 of Matthew's Gospel is dominated by the magi from the East and their positive response to the revelation of the birth of the King of the Jews. This chapter opens in Bethlehem and closes in Nazareth, the two main sites in the hidden life of Jesus.[5] In the second part of Matthew's chapter 2, Joseph takes the Holy Family away from Bethlehem for their safety to an area at least controlled by Egypt, where they stayed for an undetermined period. Movement from then on is toward Nazareth, the city of Christ's boyhood. This chapter closes by identifying the geographic place, Nazareth, with the fulfillment of scripture: "There he [Joseph] made his home in a town called Nazareth, so that what had been spoken through the prophets might be fulfilled, 'He will be called a Nazorean.'" (Mt 2:23). Interestingly, the Old Testament location for that quote cannot be found.[6]

Jesus of Nazareth

We now turn to Nazareth to visit the town as it is today and try to envision the area and the milieu as it was in the time of Jesus. Obviously this is a difficult task and one that cannot be done perfectly. But the attempt is worth the effort. Details may be scanty, but the general contour of the town and its surroundings remain essentially the same. In a country as small as New Jersey, distances between regions are not far from one another. Traveling from Jerusalem to Nazareth in modern times does not take long—perhaps three or four hours at most. Heading for the town where Jesus grew up, the visitor crosses the broad green valley of Esdraelon, with every mountain and hill reminiscent of Christ's boyhood. As a young man he must have climbed the slopes behind Nazareth very often. There he could gaze out over the magnificent panorama with the valley stretching north toward the Sea of Galilee and the Golan Heights.[7]

Not much about those youthful years is related in the New Testament. "The child grew and became strong, filled with wisdom; and the favor of God was upon him" (Lk 2:40). Like any other young man, Jesus developed gradually through childhood and young manhood. From what we know, the son of Mary looked no different from the sons of other mothers in Nazareth—much like the children one sees playing there in the streets today. As any other child he grew not only physically but intellectually and psychologically. Along with his developing faculties, his experiential knowledge also evolved. He learned language and his future craft with Joseph. He spoke Aramaic, the language of those about him, and used Hebrew in the synagogue, which he faithfully attended on the sabbath. Probably he knew some Greek as well. He did not merely have the appearance of being human; he was *really* human.

To capture the atmosphere of Christ's boyhood in Nazareth, to try to recreate those images, the modern visitor must wander about through its narrow cobblestone streets, winding and twisting then even as they do today. One must hear the sounds of children playing, laughing; listen to the hawkers selling their wares; hear the bells from the Basilica of the Annunciation. And not least, one must peer into the open doors of a craftsman's workshop, perhaps a woodworker with a youthful apprentice, mindful of how it was with Joseph and his young son learning the trade. Most likely Joseph would have been a familiar sight in a small village like Nazareth. Matthew refers to Jesus as the son of a "carpenter," which probably meant a general contractor. There was no word in Hebrew for *carpenter* as we use the word today; Joseph was probably an all-purpose builder who worked with many different materials: wood, stone, metal. In such a small, rustic country village the handiwork of such a craftsman was very important, indeed indispensable. In later years, when Jesus returned to the place of his boyhood, he was rejected as being too much like any other young man of the village. "Where did this man get this wisdom and these deeds of power? Is not this the carpenter's son? Is not his mother called Mary?"(Mt 13:54–55).

Of course, the Nazareth of Christ's time no longer remains; but there is no question that the location of the modern city rests on the ancient site. Guidebooks point out devotional spots such as Mary's well, Saint Joseph's carpenter shop, the synagogue Jesus attended on the Sabbath—even the precipice from which the villagers on one occasion were about to throw Christ—all are dubious at best. Only the grotto under the Basilica of the Annunciation has anything resembling archaeological support.

In Nazareth we are told that Joseph, Mary, and Jesus lived in a "house"—a word that we might imagine does not mean exactly the same as today. A typical home at the time of Christ was a rudimentary affair, a simple whitewashed cube with few openings, often none except for the door. Everything inside was more or less dark, requiring the use of an oil lamp, probably one of those squat clay types with a short handle, the kind so plentiful from archaeological digs in the Middle East. Lamps are prominent in the Gospels for both their practical as well as their symbolic function. Some houses were partly cave dwellings built up against a cliffside, with an additional room hollowed out.

Like other boys his age, the young Jesus went to a school connected with the synagogue when he was about five years of age. In this setting children sat on the ground around the master (often the rabbi); their principal task was to repeat by rote in unison what the master said out loud. The object of learning, the one book used, was the Torah; in fact, everything else—history, geography, language, grammar and the like—all were learned in connection with the study of this sacred book. Here, of course, Hebrew was taught, since that language and not Aramaic was used in the synagogue.

The Basilica of the Annunciation

Based on early Jewish-Christian tradition, the section of Nazareth where the Holy Family lived was in the old part of the town, where the hills come together forming a kind of hollow known as lower Nazareth. The population now is a mixture of Christian and Muslim. Over this area rises the enormous Franciscan Basilica of the Annunciation dominating the whole town, the largest Christian edifice in Israel. The church, completed in 1968, marks the site where tradition holds that the Archangel Gabriel announced to Mary that she was to become the mother of God. When the basilica was constructed, special care was taken to preserve the ancient grotto that had been incorporated into earlier churches. Markings in stone gave evidence that the site was revered by the early Jewish-Christian community dating back to the first century A.D. Before construction began, an extensive archaeological search of the whole area was undertaken. According to archaeologists, the examination was so thorough that not one square centimeter of ground was left unexplored, making it the most completely documented of all the sanctuaries in the Holy Land. Among the findings was a stone carved with the letters: XE MAPIA or "Hail Mary"—an inscription written before A.D. 431, the year when at the Council of Ephesus Mary was officially declared to be "Mother of God."[8]

At the same location, in 427 a Byzantine church was built, followed by a Crusader structure in the twelfth century. Parts of the latter are still visible today. In fact, the new basilica followed the essential lines of the Crusader church of the Middle Ages. In a word, the Basilica of the Annunciation blends together Judaeo-Christian, Byzantine, and Crusader remains recovered from archaeological excavations. In essence there are two superimposed churches: the lower one, or crypt where the grotto is preserved, and the upper structure, used as a parish church, dominated by an imposing central dome. On both levels light filtering through magnificent stained glass windows celebrates for us the joy of the Annunciation.

Mount Tabor: The Transfiguration

Less than a thirty-minute drive from Nazareth, cone-shaped Mount Tabor rises straight up from the flat valley floor. From every direction it can be seen for miles. At the foot of the mountain taxis are available for the ascent to the summit. The narrow mountain road is steep, winding, and full of hairpin curves that drivers seem to delight to tackle at full speed. Some visitors prefer to hike up to the top, but it is an arduous and often very warm climb. Awaiting the traveler at the summit is a breathtaking panoramic view. Stretching far into the distance is the Jezreel Valley, Israel's richest and most fertile farming area. Checkerboard patterns of golden wheat, fields of green vegetables, black rich earth, vineyards, and fruit trees combine to form a colorful quilt as far as the eye can see.[9]

Not only is the location of Mount Tabor spectacular, but it has about it a certain aura that suggests the sacred. Early tradition selected it as the site of the Transfiguration of Jesus narrated in the Gospel: "Six days later, Jesus took with him Peter and James and his brother John and led them up a high mountain, by themselves. And he was transfigured before them, and his face shone like the sun, and his clothes became dazzling white" (Mt 17:1–2). A cloud appeared over them and a voice was heard saying, "This is my Son, the Beloved; with him I am well pleased; listen to him!" (Mt 17:5).

As scripture scholar Raymond Brown observes, the identity of Jesus as God's son is proclaimed here again as it was at his baptism. "But the disciples were not present at that time," says Brown. "Thus far in the public ministry no follower of Jesus has made a believing confession of that identity. Now…the heavenly voice re-identifies Jesus." A primary purpose for this extraordinary happening is to prepare and strengthen the three apostles for Christ's passion and death to come. This is underscored by their conversation on the way down the mountain with the prediction that the Son of Man must suffer but will rise from the dead.[10]

Controversy regarding the site of the Transfiguration can be found among early Christian writers. Some have suggested the rather improbable Mount Hermon, a snow-capped (ten-thousand-foot) peak far north in Lebanon as the site. Finally, Cyril of Jerusalem (an early Father of the Church) settled on Mount Tabor, which was confirmed by Jerome, translator of the vulgate (Latin) Bible.[11]

Just when the first religious structure appeared on the mountain is not certain. Ruins of several ancient churches and monasteries (especially Benedictine) can be seen on the summit today, some dating from Byzantine and Crusader periods. At one time the Benedictines turned their monastery into a fortress for protection against invading Turkish armies. The fortress-monastery ceased to exist after the defeat of the Crusaders at the Horns of Hattin near Tiberias in 1187.

Today the most prominent structure on Mount Tabor is the Franciscan church built in the 1920s—one of the most beautiful churches in the Holy Land. Constructed on two levels, well-placed windows allow brilliant sunlight to stream through, suggesting the Transfiguration described in the Gospel. At either side of the entrance to the huge structure are two chapels, one dedicated to Moses and the other to Elijah, commemorating their presence in the Transfiguration appearance described by Matthew, who again uses semitic parallelism. As God spoke to Moses on Mount Sinai, so again he speaks on Mount Tabor. The presence of Elijah suggests an early Christian understanding coupling him with John the Baptist: "But I tell you that Elijah has already come, and they did not recognize him, but did to him whatever they pleased" (Mt 17:12).

Deborah Crushed the Canaanites

Mount Tabor not only appears prominently in the New Testament, but it is also the dramatic scene of ancient Jewish events as well. In the area around the foot of Mount Tabor, the Old Testament tells of fierce battles that were once waged between the tribes of Israel and their Canaanite enemies narrated in the Book of Judges.

During the time when "there was no king in Israel; all the people did what was right in their own eyes" (Judg 21:25). Unfortunately this did not always work so well! Without a single leader, the tribes of Israel were so disorganized that the Canaanites beat them up. It became evident that what Israelites needed was a charismatic individual who could bring unity and order to the tribes. Such a one was

Deborah, who was a prophetess and a "Judge." In this time of crisis, Deborah was the person; Mount Tabor was the place.

She gathered the tribes on Mount Tabor, gave instructions and inspiration to Barak, the chosen general, and launched what proved to be the total defeat of the opposing Canaanites led by Sisera. "Deborah said to Barak, 'Up! For this is the day on which the LORD has given Sisera into your hand. The LORD indeed is going out before you.' So Barak went down from Mount Tabor with ten thousand warriors following him" (Judg 4:14).

"When Sisera was told that Barak...had gone up to Mount Tabor, Sisera called out all his chariots, nine hundred chariots of iron, and all the troops who were with him" (Judg 4:12). But to no avail! The tribes of Israel now united by Deborah swooped down from Mount Tabor and defeated the Canaanites, who were literally "stuck in the mud." Sisera dismounted from his chariot and fled on foot in the drenching rain with Barak in hot pursuit. Sisera then made the fatal mistake of accepting the invitation of the Israelite woman, Jael, to rest in her tent. She gave him milk, covered him with a rug, then as he slept she drove a tent pin through his head into the ground, abruptly ending his military career. When Barak appeared, he found Sisera already dead.

In typical ancient Hebrew tradition, a song of victory, the "Canticle of Deborah," was sung, which ended with: "So perish all your enemies O Lord! / But may your friends be like the sun as it rises in its might" (Judg 5:31).

In the area around Nazareth, a region so related to events of Jewish history, Jesus lived most of his life. In fact, all of his so-called hidden life was lived here, before he began his public ministry. The hills around Nazareth and stories such as Deborah on Mount Tabor must have been recalled in his many walks about the countryside of Galilee. Added to this was simply the natural beauty of this part of Palestine.

Few countries of the world have so much diversity in so small an area. In just an hour a walk will take one from the richest of plains to hills where sheep graze and camel caravans dip and rise not far from the shadow of snow-capped Mount Hermon. Such is the land from which Jesus came and that he left to offer the supreme sacrifice for humankind.

As stated in the introduction to this book, our purpose had been to try to relate the life of Jesus to the actual sites. Unfortunately little is known about those thirty years in Nazareth, even though they cover the greater part of Jesus' life. To try to recapture the place, context, and background is an effort by its nature drastically limited. As least the attempt may help one to contemplate more deeply the meaning of scripture: "The Word became flesh and dwelt among us" in a specific time and place in history.

The Annunciation

In the sixth month the angel Gabriel was sent by God to a town...called Nazareth, to a virgin engaged to a man whose name was Joseph, of the house of David. The virgin's name was Mary. And he came to her and said, "Greetings, favored one! The Lord is with you." But she was much perplexed by his words and pondered what sort of greeting this might be. The angel said to her, "Do not be afraid, Mary, for you have found favor with God. And now you will conceive in your womb and bear a son, and you will name him Jesus. He will be great, and will be called the Son of the Most High, and the Lord God will give him the throne of his ancestor David. He will reign over the house of Jacob forever, and of his kingdom there will be no end." Mary said to the angel, "How can this be, since I am a virgin?" The angel said to her, "The Holy Spirit will come upon you, and the power of the Most High will overshadow you; therefore the child to be born will be holy; he will be called Son of God. And now your relative Elizabeth in her old age has also conceived a son; and this is the sixth month for her who was said to be barren. For nothing will be impossible with God." Then Mary said, "Here I am, the servant of the Lord; let it be with me according to your word." Then the angel departed from her. (Lk 1:26–38)

Fig. 30 Basilica of the Annunciation. The Basilica of the Annunciation was built over the traditional site where the Archangel Gabriel announced to Mary that she was to become the mother of God.

Photo by Lorna Patterson

Photo by Chris Yaniger

Fig. 31 Grotto of the Annunciation. The grotto of the Annunciation is preserved with ancient inscriptions, archaeological evidence that early Christian pilgrims came to revere the site as still is done today. The largest Christian church in the Holy Land, the basilica was completed in 1968.

The Birth of Jesus

In those days a decree went out from Emperor Augustus that all the world should be registered. This was the first registration and was taken while Quirinius was governor of Syria. All went to their own towns to be registered. Joseph also went from the town of Nazareth in Galilee to Judea, to the city of David called Bethlehem, because he was descended from the house and family of David. He went to be registered with Mary, to whom he was engaged and who was expecting a child. While they were there, the time came for her to deliver her child. And she gave birth to her firstborn son and wrapped him in bands of cloth, and laid him in a manger, because there was no place for them in the inn.

In that region there were shepherds living in the fields, keeping watch over their flock by night. Then an angel of the Lord stood before them, and the glory of the Lord shone around them, and they were terrified. But the angel said to them, "Do not be afraid; for see—I am bringing you good news of great joy for all the people: to you is born this day in the city of David a Savior, who is the Messiah, the Lord. This will be a sign for you: you will find a child wrapped in bands of cloth and lying in a manger." And suddenly there was with the angel a multitude of the heavenly host, praising God and saying,

"Glory to God in the highest heaven,
and on earth peace among those whom he favors!"

When the angels had left them and gone into heaven, the shepherds said to one another, "Let us go now to Bethlehem and see this thing that has taken place, which the Lord has made known to us." So they went with haste and found Mary and Joseph, and the child lying in the manger. When they saw this, they made known what had been told them about this child; and all who heard it were amazed at what the shepherds told them. But Mary treasured all these words and pondered them in her heart. (Lk 2:1-19)

Fig. 32 Basilica of the Nativity. The Basilica of the Nativity was dedicated by Emperor Constantine in A.D. 339 and rebuilt by Emperor Justinian in the sixth century. At the far end is the high altar flanked by columns. Beneath, accessible by steps on either side, is the cave revered by Christians as the place of Christ's birth.

Photo by Lorna Patterson

Photo by Lorna Patterson

Fig. 33 Traditional site of Christ's birth. The silver star marks the traditional site of Christ's birth.

83

The Transfiguration

Six days later, Jesus took with him Peter and James and his brother John and led them up a high mountain, by themselves. And he was transfigured before them, and his face shone like the sun, and his clothes became dazzling white. Suddenly there appeared to them Moses and Elijah, talking with him. Then Peter said to Jesus, "Lord, it is good for us to be here; if you wish, I will make three dwellings here, one for you, one for Moses, and one for Elijah." While he was still speaking, suddenly a bright cloud overshadowed them, and from the cloud a voice said, "This is my Son, the Beloved; with him I am well pleased; listen to him!" When the disciples heard this, they fell to the ground and were overcome by fear. But Jesus came and touched them, saying, "Get up and do not be afraid." And when they looked up, they saw no one except Jesus himself alone.

As they were coming down the mountain, Jesus ordered them, "Tell no one about the vision until after the Son of Man has been raised from the dead." And the disciples asked him, "Why, then do the scribes say that Elijah must come first?" He replied, "Elijah is indeed coming and will restore all things; but I tell you that Elijah has already come, and they did not recognize him, but they did to him whatever they pleased. So also the Son Man is about to suffer at their hands." Then the disciples understood that he was speaking to them about John the Baptist. (Mt 17:1–13)

Photographer Unknown

Fig. 34 Basilica of the Transfiguration. With a superb view of the Jezreel Valley, the Basilica of Transfiguration stands atop Mount Tabor. Since the fourth century, Christian tradition has identified this as the site where Jesus was transfigured before Peter, James, and John. Italian architect Antonio Barluzzi built the church in the 1920s over a former Byzantine basilica. Both the outstanding mosaics and the interior of the building itself wonderfully capture the spirit of the event and its spectacular location.

Notes

1. Burri, Rene, *H. V. Morton: In Search of the Holy Land*, New York: Dodd, Mead and Co. (1979), p. 17. About images of the Nativity, H. V. Morton observes, "Every Christian nation has translated the story of Christ into its own idiom and cradled him in its own barns. The great medieval painters, each man in his own way, painted in the national background of his own country and his own time. And we who come from Europe come from an enchanted country to the bare rocks and crags of reality."

2. Brown, Raymond, *The Birth of the Messiah*, New York: Doubleday (1979), pp. 515–16. Bethlehem as the birthplace of Jesus certainly is universal in Christian tradition. Brown's discussion of the birthplace of Jesus concludes, "The evidence, thus, for the birthplace in Bethlehem is much weaker than the evidence for the Davidic descent or even evidence for a virginal conception; and these three Christian claims are not necessarily interdependent."

3. Fitzmyer, Joseph A., S.J., *The Gospel According to Luke*, vol. I, New York: Doubleday (1985), p. 31. Certain nuances ought to be noted in the light of modern scholarship. Fitzmyer observes that the "setting for the birth of Jesus (Lk 2:1–5) describes the edict for a worldwide census issued by Augustus.... It is clear that the census is purely a literary device used by him to associate Mary and Joseph, residents of Nazareth, with Bethlehem, the town of David because he knows of a tradition, also attested in Matthew, that Jesus was born in Bethlehem."

4. Murphy-O'Connor, Jerome, O.P., *The Holy Land: An Archaeological Guide*, New York: Oxford University Press (1998), p. 201.

5. Brown, *Birth of the Messiah*, p. 178.

6. Murphy-O'Connor, *Holy Land*, p. 374. Commentators observe that it is not clear where Mary and Joseph lived before the birth of Jesus. "Matthew implies that it was Bethlehem (Matt. 2) but Luke says that it was Nazareth (Lk. 2:4-5). It is more probable that Matthew is correct: Joseph belonged to a Judean family. Were Nazareth their home it would have been more natural to return there when Herod menaced the family than to go to Egypt. Judeans, on the other hand, automatically thought of Egypt as a place of refuge (I Kgs. II, 40; 2 Kgs. 25; Jer. 26, 21)."

7. At the time of Christ, Nazareth was only a village, one little known even in Galilee. It is not even mentioned in the Old Testament. Today

it is a large town, entirely Arab and divided between Christians and Muslims. Overlooking Nazareth today on a nearby hill is Nazareth Illit or Upper Nazareth, a Jewish settlement founded in 1957.

8. Hoade, Eugene, O.F.M., *Guide to the Holy Land*, Jerusalem: Franciscan Printing Press (1973), p. 691. Ancient artifacts including inscriptions can be seen in the museum beside the Basilica of the Annunciation. The "Mary" inscription is the oldest of its kind, written before devotion to Mary became universal. Among the graffiti another inscription reads, "Christ, Son of God." This throws light on the beliefs of the first Christians of Nazareth, who were of Jewish origin.

9. Those who write about Mount Tabor can hardly restrain their enthusiasm when describing its unique beauty. The following quotes are graphic examples: "On account of its graceful form, its picturesque site, its striking vegetation and the splendor of its panorama, it stands out among all the mountains of Palestine" (Hoade, *Guide to the Holy Land*, p. 706). "The perfect breast shape of Mount Tabor excites awe and wonder; it has the aura of a sacred mountain. From the dawn of history it was a place where humanity found contact with the numinous and it is hardly surprising that Christian tradition eventually located there the transfiguration of Jesus" (Murphy-O'Connor, *Holy Land*, p. 366).

10. Brown, Raymond, *An Introduction to the New Testament*, New York: Doubleday (1996), p. 139. Brown also notes that the scene takes place on a mountain amidst the presence of Elijah and Moses, who encountered God on Mount Sinai. These Old Testament figures are represented in beautiful scenes in chapels that grace each side of the entrance to the basilica.

11. Buttrick, George (ed.), *The Interpreter's Bible*, vol. 4, New York: Abingdon Press (1962), p. 508. Mount Tabor is not named in the Gospels as the site of the Transfiguration. Because of this, the site cannot be identified with absolute certainty. But the Transfiguration itself is narrated in all three Synoptic Gospels (Mt 17:1–8; Mk 9:2–8; Lk 9:28–36).

Chapter 4
THE GRECO-ROMAN WORLD

Photo by Lorna Patterson

Fig. 35 Bet Shean. At the time of Christ, Greco-Roman cities existed all over Palestine. Bet Shean in Galilee, shown, is still under excavation and restoration. Awareness of these cities helps to visualize the setting in which the gospel events occurred. Mention is frequently made in the New Testament of the Decapolis, ten Greek cities founded in the Holy Land after the time of Alexander the Great.

Map 8
GRECO-ROMAN PALESTINE

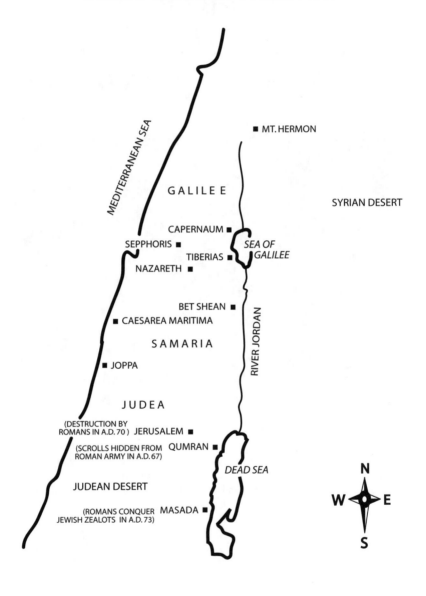

MT. HERMON ■

MEDITERRANEAN SEA

GALILEE

SYRIAN DESERT

CAPERNAUM ■

SEPPHORIS ■

SEA OF GALILEE

TIBERIAS ■

NAZARETH ■

BET SHEAN ■

RIVER JORDAN

■ CAESAREA MARITIMA

SAMARIA

■ JOPPA

JUDEA

(DESTRUCTION BY ROMANS IN A.D. 70) JERUSALEM ■

(SCROLLS HIDDEN FROM ROMAN ARMY IN A.D. 67) QUMRAN ■

DEAD SEA

JUDEAN DESERT

(ROMANS CONQUER JEWISH ZEALOTS IN A.D. 73) MASADA ■

N
W ◆ E
S

To get the full impact of the biblical story, one needs contact with the physical and cultural background that informs it. Jesus was born, lived, and died within the historical-cultural context of the Greco-Roman world as well as in the Jewish world. It was not a world that simply surrounded him; rather he entered into it, was a part of it, and moved about within its context. Knowledge of this serves to help us vitalize the setting in which Jesus lived and in which the gospel events occurred, making the pages of the New Testament come alive. Likewise, the tiny new Christian community grew within the same milieu. It not only existed within Greco-Roman culture, but also bore witness to a new phase of the empire's destructive power. So we begin with the Roman capital in Palestine, Caesarea Maritima.

Caesarea by the Sea

North of Tel Aviv on the Mediterranean coast are the remains of Herod the Great's once-mighty seaport—Caesarea Maritima. Little is left today. Rolling waves dash over half-sunken columns as breakers crash on the sandy shore and then quietly recede while the surf readies itself to bombard the shore again.

Long ago this once-spectacular artificial harbor sank in an earthquake, and the Mediterranean rushed in to hide the ruins from view. But at the height of its activity, Caesarea was the pride of Herod's handiwork, Rome's showplace in the Middle East. Dominating the harbor was a temple dedicated to Caesar Augustus and a gigantic statue of Caesar himself.[1]

According to Jewish historian Flavius Josephus, Herod used extraordinary measures to construct his harbor—definitely "state of the art" for his time. To build breakwaters against southern storms arising from Egypt, Josephus writes that Herod sank huge stone blocks into the ocean. However, underwater archaeologists using scuba diving equipment have found no evidence of the gigantic stone blocks that were described. Instead the remains of wooden frames filled with hydraulic cement that hardens under water were found. Modern engineers view this technique as quite astonishing considering that the construction was completed more than two thousand years ago. Nevertheless, most of what Josephus wrote has proven to be an invaluable and usually reliable source of information for scholars. In many cases his is the only eyewitness account.[2]

An example is the description he gives of the building of the harbor and the city center around it in only twelve years—a record time in that day and age. Gangs of workmen and slaves worked around the clock to complete the enormous task. Warehouses and temples were built, grid systems for streets laid out, water and sewage facilities installed. Even a hippodrome for chariot races and an amphitheater overlooking the Mediterranean were included. Perhaps the most dramatic achievement (still standing) was a two-story aqueduct that brought water from Mount Carmel, more than eight miles away.[3]

Evidence of Pontius Pilate in Caesarea

That Caesarea was not only a busy seaport but also the Roman political center of Palestine is clear from both written and archaeological evidence. Near the theater was found a stone tablet inscribed with the name Pontius Pilate, the only archaeological evidence outside of the Bible of the Roman magistrate who condemned Christ to death. A replica of the stone now stands on the site of discovery. Inscribed in Latin, the translated version reads, "Pontius Pilate, Prefect of Judea, made and dedicated the Tiberieum to Divine Augustus." Interesting to note is that Pilate's title here is Prefect, not Procurator as he is usually known. Apparently the stone originally belonged to a shrine dedicated to the deified Emperor Tiberius.[4]

Whether Pontius Pilate should be called procurator or prefect is of no real significance, since in practice the authority was about the same. His was a key function between the Roman emperor and the high priest in Israel—a delicate balancing act to be sure. Perhaps the best illustration of this is the trial of Jesus, when Pilate was caught between pleasing both the high priest in Jerusalem and Caesar in Rome.

Although Rome ostensibly ruled Judea at the time of Christ, the framework of the Jewish political world was left essentially intact—a unique arrangement among countries dominated by Rome. Even though Romans reigned, the political structure was left substantially in place. A subjugated region was either made into a new Roman province or incorporated into one already existing. In this case, Judea was annexed to the province of Syria.

To such an annexed territory, the emperor sent a procurator or prefect under whom the traditional political structure was substantially preserved. Such was the situation with Judea and Pontius Pilate. Rome was ultimately in charge; however, at the head of the nation still remained the high priest.

Rome never deviated from its policy of respecting the religious institutions in place in conquered countries, even adapting to their laws, customs, and sometimes their particular biases and prejudices. Jews in Palestine could not be called into court on the Sabbath and were exempt from military service. Out of respect for the Jewish prohibition against graven images, Roman soldiers were not allowed to bring emblems of Caesar into Jerusalem. An insight into how Rome and the judicial system worked together can be seen in the next section of the chapter, in which we provide Luke's detailed narration of Paul's position, caught between Roman authority and the Sanhedrin, the Jewish legal-religious council.

Peter and Paul in Caesarea

As far as we know, Jesus himself never visited Caesarea. Peter, however, did so soon after Pentecost. In fact, it was at Caesarea that Peter, spokesman for the twelve, began to inaugurate the mission to the

Gentiles, a critical development for this completely Jewish community. In a lengthy episode, Luke recounts how Peter was summoned by God to Caesarea to baptize Cornelius, a Roman centurion of the Italian Cohort (Acts 10:1).

The conversion of Cornelius at Caesarea is of great importance because it set a precedent for the admission of Gentiles into the church, in total disregard of Old Testament law. Luke underscores the significance of the event by repetition. The vision of Cornelius is recounted four times. God's revelation to Peter that a Gentile may indeed be baptized (despite Peter's objection) is told twice, and finally Peter repeats and summarizes the whole story (Acts 11:5–18). The importance Luke gives the Cornelius event is underscored by the fact that he devotes to it nearly two chapters. This episode is not simply another conversion story like the baptism of the Ethiopian by Philip (Acts 8:26–40). As presented by Luke, all the action is initiated and directed by God. The scene opens in Caesarea with "a man named Cornelius, a centurion of the Italian Cohort….He was a devout man who feared God with all his household" (Acts 10:1–2).

One afternoon during prayer Cornelius heard a voice saying, "Send some men to Joppa for a certain Simon who is called Peter" (Acts 10:5). The next day the scene changes to Joppa, a town on the Mediterranean (near today's Tel Aviv). There, while staying with Simon the tanner, Peter went up on the roof to pray. While so engaged he fell into a trance, during which he experienced a vision. He saw the heavens open, and a large sheet came down containing animals of all kinds. Since he felt hungry and wanted something to eat the animals looked good indeed; however he recoiled from them when he took a closer look. We assume that some were forbidden by Jewish dietary laws. Peter in his typical spontaneous style replied to the command "Kill and eat" with an immediate and strong rejection: "By no means, Lord: for I have never eaten anything that is profane or unclean" (Acts 10:14).[5]

The command was given three times, until Peter finally relented. While he was still reflecting on the meaning of the vision, the delegates sent by Cornelius from Caesarea arrived in Joppa. At their bidding Peter then went to Caesarea. Upon reaching Cornelius's house he finds his host and all his household waiting.

> On Peter's arrival Cornelius met him, and falling at his feet, worshiped him. But Peter made him get up, saying, "Stand up! I am only a mortal." And as he talked with him, he went in and found that many had assembled; and he said to them, "You yourselves know that it is unlawful for a Jew to associate with or visit with a Gentile, but God has shown me that I should not call anyone profane or unclean.... Now may I ask why you sent for me?" (Acts 10:25–29)

Cornelius recounted his vision and explained why he had sent messengers to Joppa for Peter. Peter then began to speak to them, saying, "I truly understand that God shows no partiality, but in every nation anyone who fears him and does what is right is acceptable to him" (Acts 10:34–35). Thereupon Peter recounts how he had come to understand this through the message God had given to him in the apparition.

Of course, the vision was highly symbolic. At first its meaning seemed to be instruction about food: nothing was profane or unclean. Beneath this symbolism, however, Peter finally grasped the deeper meaning concerning all mankind, that none have been left beyond the pale of salvation. While Peter was explaining this, the Holy Spirit fell upon all who were present, including the Gentiles. The Jewish believers who had come with Peter were astounded that the gift of the Holy Spirit had been given even to the Gentiles. At this point Peter said to them, "'Can anyone withhold the water for baptizing these people who have received the Holy Spirit as we have?' So he ordered them to be baptized" (Acts 10:44).

When Jewish Christians in Judea heard of Peter's action, many were highly skeptical. Peter was called upon to justify his actions in baptizing the Gentiles, and once again the whole story of his vision is repeated. Luke, the narrator, was not present, so just where did he get all this information? It is not likely that he invented the story as a literary device; therefore he must have had at hand early tradition. Luke's main purpose is theological: to show God's plan for the salvation of humankind.

As Caesarea was the beginning of Peter's mission, for Paul it was near the end. The whole latter part of Acts of the Apostles sees Paul in Caesarea before Roman magistrates and King Agrippa, where he is held to render an account of his activities in the face of accusations by the scribes and Pharisees.

Fortunately Paul was born in Tarsus, capital of the Roman province of Cilicia in southeast Asia Minor. Everyone born in Tarsus automatically had Roman citizenship, a privilege granted by Antony and confirmed by Caesar Augustus in 31 B.C. Standing before the Roman governor, Festus, Paul used his status as a Roman citizen to escape the predicament. One cannot help but admire Paul's sense of timing. For long he desired to go to Rome; here was an opportunity for a free trip. So at the last moment he exclaimed, "I appeal to the emperor." This was his privilege as a Roman citizen. "Then Festus, after conferring with his council, replied: 'You have appealed to the emperor; to the emperor you will go'" (Acts 25:11–12).[6]

In a ship setting out from Caesarea, Paul eventually arrives in Rome and is kept prisoner; then according to tradition he was beheaded on the Appian Way outside of Rome, a site now marked by the basilica St. Paul's Outside the Walls. The year was A.D. 64, during the persecution of the Emperor Nero. The narrative ends abruptly; Paul's death is not reported in Acts. Luke, the author of Acts, seems to feel he has brought his narrative theme to its conclusion once Paul is finally in Rome. He has shown how the apostolic testimony was carried to the "ends of the earth," since Rome was the center of the known civilized world at that time. "You will be my witnesses in Jerusalem, in all Judea and Samaria, and to the ends of the earth" (Acts 1:8). Although Caesarea is not generally thought of as a "sacred site," the city played an important role early on in the spread of Christianity.[7]

Rome's Domination: Pompey's Conquest

Rome's power and influence in Palestine began long before the time of Christ. Roman general Pompey had taken the first critical step in the area following in the wake of Alexander the Great's conquest of the Middle East. Hellenistic or Greek presence was already quite visible at the time Pompey and his army swooped down upon Palestine. Semitic tribes in the ancient Middle East had never seen anything like it before. The vision of marching legions, Roman eagles mounted on approaching standards, their weapons and discipline all combined to form a striking and formidable scene. Although these desert tribes had viewed armies before, never had they been so overwhelmed as by Pompey's impressive army sweeping relentlessly down the Jordan Valley.[8]

With the coming of Pompey a new era was introduced in the Middle East. Now everything Greek was the "in thing." Among the enthusiasts was Israel's puppet king, Herod. In Jerusalem he had a hippodrome built for chariot racing and incorporated Greek architecture in the Royal Portico of the Temple. At the same time he was building a temple in Samaria at Sebaste for pagan sacrifices. Outwardly Herod pretended to be a Jew but inwardly he was not. It was Rome that gave him the illusion of power; and it was Rome that used him for its own purposes. Both promoted Greco-Roman civilization in Palestine. Such is the background of the region in which the Gospel story took place.

Sepphoris:
A Greco-Roman City near Nazareth

Four miles from Nazareth, scarcely an hour's walk away, is the Greco-Roman city of Sepphoris. In the time of Jesus it could easily be seen from Nazareth, seated as it was high on a mountain. For that reason it originally got the name Zippori, which in Hebrew means "bird." Like a bird on its lofty perch, Sepphoris commanded a bird's-eye view of the surrounding countryside. Most likely for that reason it grew into a fortified city, a watchtower against invasions by the Egyptians from the south.[9]

Plying their trade as carpenters and general building contractors, Joseph and his son Jesus probably visited the city, though we have no record of it. A thriving city such as Sepphoris had need of such skilled craftsmen; Joseph and Jesus may have been in demand. As New Testament scholar Joseph Fitzmyer has observed, Joseph's family did not come from the lowest stratum of Palestinian society but were skilled craftsmen who filled an important need in that day and age.

How much influence did predominantly Gentile cities such as Sepphoris have on the Nazareth of Jesus' time? Given their proximity, some communication would have been possible. Excavations in Sepphoris (still in progress) reveal as well that the city was not entirely Greco-Roman (and Greek speaking) as previously thought but contained a Jewish population as well. Nazareth has yielded very few archaeological remains, so to understand the Galilee of Jesus' time, attention has been given to the city closest to it. The hope is that the excavations at Sepphoris can also shed some light on the area in general at the time when Jesus was growing up.

Clearly Sepphoris had a mixed population. The large number of Jews seemed to have existed side by side with the Gentile population. Although the Greek language was predominant, Hebrew was also spoken. And on occasion conflicts broke out, as Josephus narrates in his

Wars of the Jews: "In Sepphoris, a city of Galilee, there was one Judas.... This man got no small multitude together and broke into the place where the armor was laid up and attacked those that were so earnest to gain the dominion...."[10]

This rebellion was short-lived and easily put down by the Romans. But the incident reveals something about this city: it was divided. And it was not completely in the hands of the Gentiles, even though Hellenism was spreading in this region at the time of Christ.

Since it is on two main highways running from north to south, Sepphoris grew into an important commercial center on a busy trading route. Also, it became a center of Jewish learning in the first century A.D. Here was the Sanhedrin, the highest Jewish court; and here the Mishnah, earliest and most basic rabbinic text, was first compiled.

Bringing water to the city was a problem because of its high elevation. Archaeologists have found an abundance of cisterns, channels, and an aqueduct more than eight miles long. Many small baths have been uncovered among the ruins; scholars, however, are divided over whether they were used for personal hygiene or for ritual baths.

In this city so close to Nazareth both Jewish and Greco-Roman cultures flourished in the first century A.D. In a magnificent villa just south of Sepphoris, discoveries dating from the fourth century A.D. have caused quite a stir of interest among scholars. One of the well-preserved colorful mosaics is an exquisite portrait of a beautiful young woman who has come to be known as the "Mona Lisa of Galilee."[11]

Bet Shean

Southeast of Nazareth at the edge of the Jordan Valley are additional Greco-Roman ruins still under excavation. The city, Bet Shean, is the most extensive of all the Greco-Roman remains discovered in Israel. Located on an ancient busy trade route, it was continuously occupied for more than six thousand years. In the eighteenth century B.C.,

Egyptian forces used it as a military outpost, followed in the thirteenth century B.C. by Israel's tribe of Manasseh, which took over this part of the divided Canaanite territory. But later, in a fierce battle, the Philistines conquered the region, slaying King Saul and his sons, whose bodies were hung on the walls of Bet Shean. Saul had been an enemy of David, but out of respect for one who was a former king, the Israelites came by night, took down the bodies, and buried them under cover of darkness (I Sam I:17).

One of the most moving canticles in the Old Testament is the lament of David over the death of Saul and especially his son Jonathan, whom David loved very much:

> Your glory, O Israel, lies slain upon your high places!
>   How the mighty have fallen!
> Tell it not...
>   in the streets of Ashkelon;
> or the daughters of the Philistines will rejoice,
>   the daughters of the uncircumcised will exult.
>
> You mountains of Gilboa,
>   let there be no dew or rain upon you,
>   nor bounteous fields!
> For there the shield of the mighty was defiled,
>   and the shield of Saul, anointed with oil no more...
>
> Saul and Jonathan, beloved and lovely!
>   In life and in death they were not divided;
> they were swifter than eagles,
>   they were stronger than lions.
>
> O daughters of Israel, weep over Saul...
>   ornaments of gold on your apparel.
>
> How the mighty have fallen
>   in the midst of battle!

Jonathan lies slain upon your high places.

I am distressed for you, my brother Jonathan;
greatly beloved were you to me;

your love to me was wonderful,
passing the love of women.

How the mighty have fallen,
and the weapons of war perished! (2 Sam 1:19–21; 23–27)

Rome's conquering general Pompey (106–48 B.C.) made Bet
Shean part of the Decapolis, intending it to be a center for the spread
of Greek civilization in Palestine. Extensive ongoing excavations and
restorations have made it the most spectacular Greco-Roman site in
present-day Israel. Included among the structures so far uncovered are
a very wide *cardo* (main street), a temple, the ever-present baths, and the
best-preserved Roman amphitheater found in the country. Byzantine
courtyards, mosaics, and a basilica dating from the fifth and sixth centuries have also been found.[12]

At most excavation sites one can find archaeologists on hands
and knees painstakingly sifting through dust and dirt. With small
pickax and whiskbroom (seldom any heavy equipment), they carefully
examine a small area looking for artifacts. Not so at Bet Shean, where
the visitor comes upon huge noisy Caterpillars puffing and straining
to move tons of earth, even boulders and trees. This Greco-Roman
city, completely buried in an earthquake, could only be uncovered by
using such extraordinary measures. An enormous hill of mud had covered over the entire site.

Greco-Roman cities such as Bet Shean extended into Palestine at
the time of Christ. Some were part of the Decapolis, the ten Greco-
Roman cities mentioned by Matthew and Mark. Several were founded
by the generals that followed Alexander the Great. The Ptolemies of
Egypt and Seleucids of Syria supported them. When Pompey conquered the Near East in A.D. 63 he placed the cities of the Decapolis

under the direct rule of Rome, which pleased Herod, who found them useful for his political purposes.

In the Gospels, the region of the Decapolis (Mt 4:25; Mk 5:20; 7:31) refers to the territory in which these cities were situated; this is (roughly speaking) land east and southeast of the Sea of Galilee except

Map 9
THE DECAPOLIS

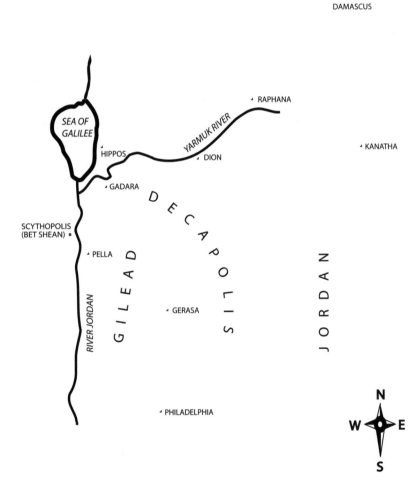

for Damascus. According to Roman historian Pliny, the ten cities orig-inally were Scythopolis (Bet Shean), Pella, Dion, Gerasa (today Jerash), Philadelphia (today Amman), Gadara, Raphana, Kanatha, Hippos, and Damascus. Names and numbers were not always constant, tending to vary with different sources.

Rome's Destructive Power

Remains of the incredible Greco-Roman civilization abound. However, in addition to spectacular architectural ruins lie evidences of ancient Rome's destructive power. Many examples exist; here three can be mentioned: Qumran (by the Dead Sea), Masada (Jewish Zealots' last stand), and ancient Jerusalem itself. From the pages of history one can visualize the dramatic scenes that led up to the complete destruc-tion of the Holy City and the Temple in A.D. 70.

In A.D. 67 Roman general Vespasian led his legions down the Jordan Valley, the region where the Jordan River meets the Dead Sea. Here the Jordan is at the lowest spot on Earth, thirteen hundred feet below sea level. Nearby is Jericho, against a backdrop of craggy barren cliffs. The Dead Sea itself is a glistening blue ribbon forty-five miles long with no outlet. Evaporation over the centuries has left this the world's saltiest body of water—nearly 34 percent salt, as compared with the 4 percent in ordinary sea water. Into this forbidding region Vespasian led his army, bent on the destruction of Jerusalem. Near Jericho, the marching legions made a sharp right turn going up to Jerusalem. Josephus tells us that around this spot at the Dead Sea, Vespasian's curiosity got the better of him. Aware of the water's salty reputation, he had a slave bound and thrown into the Dead Sea to test its legendary buoyancy. The water's reputation proved true, much to the slave's relief.

Qumran and the Dead Sea Scrolls

As the Roman army turned westward up toward Jerusalem, the tenth legion passed by Qumran, the site now famous for the Dead Sea Scroll discovery. Here some two hundred members of a Jewish religious sect called the Essenes led the communal part of their lives. They thought of themselves as the true remnant of Israel, repeating the experience of their forefathers in the days of Moses. In their view they were the elect, the "Sons of Light" who had received a new covenant.[13]

Frightened by the army's approach, the Essenes hid their library of scrolls in the surrounding cave-riddled cliffs. Here the scrolls remained hidden and unknown until discovered by accident in 1947.

In the Dead Sea Scroll discovery, both biblical and religious sectarian documents were found, some well preserved in large terra cotta Roman jars. Especially valuable were two copies of the Book of Isaiah from the second century B.C.—about nine hundred years older than any hitherto possessed. In addition to this, parts of every book of the Old Testament except the Book of Esther were discovered—literally tens of thousands of fragments. Putting them together has been the monumental task of an international ecumenical team of scholars. The cache has not yet been completely published. Acclaimed as the greatest biblical discovery of the twentieth century, the major part of the scrolls now reside in a special museum in Israel called the Shrine of the Book.

Amazingly, these Old Testament manuscripts are essentially identical with the traditional Hebrew texts handed down and still in use in the twenty-first century. All biblical scholars today consider the Dead Sea Scrolls to be invaluable. As Joseph Fitzmyer points out, "they have proven to be of immense value in the study of the history of ancient Judaism, in the study of ancient biblical languages, and especially in the examination of the Palestinian Jewish matrix of Christianity."[14]

Masada:
The Jewish Zealots' Last Stand

By far the most dramatic episode involving the Roman army was the capture of Masada, a lofty citadel rising abruptly one thousand feet above the Dead Sea. The oval-shaped flat surface boasted a spectacular three-tiered palace cascading down its northern rim, as well as an extensive Roman bath, storehouses, and water cisterns hewn out of solid rock. Additionally a second palace on the western side was discovered with magnificently preserved mosaic floors. Originally a luxury retreat of Herod, Masada was taken and transformed into a nearly impregnable fortress by Jewish Zealots who formed the last organized resistance against Rome. After a three-year siege by the Roman army camped around its base, the fortress was finally taken by General Silva, commander of the tenth legion. The year was A.D. 73.[15]

More than 960 Jewish resisters committed suicide, according to Josephus, rather than surrender to the Romans. The accuracy of this number has been called into question by recent archaeological evidence, but archaeologist Dan Bahat, who worked at the site under Yigael Yadin, considers the rest of Josephus's account accurate. The Jewish Zealots were extremist Palestinian Jews who opposed Roman occupation. Thoroughly annoyed by their guerilla attacks, the Romans were determined to crush the Zealots, and crush them they did, but it took three years.[16]

That the Zealots were an organized movement during the life of Christ is not clear; but that they were active in the uprising and rebellion against Rome is quite certain. Interestingly, one of Christ's disciples was called Simon the Zealot (Lk 6:15). They were especially strong in Galilee, where they were looking for an "anointed one" or messiah who would lead them against the Romans. For them the term *messiah* was identified with a nationalistic leader who would throw their oppressors out by force. This is why we find Jesus avoiding use of the word, especially in Mark's Gospel, saying instead "Son of Man." At the time many would have identified the word *messiah* with a political military leader.

Map 10
MASADA

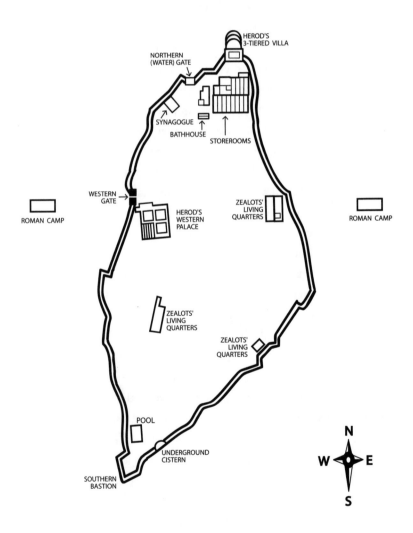

The Destruction of Jerusalem

Jerusalem's importance and theological symbolism in Hebrew scripture cannot be exaggerated. It is expressed powerfully in the Old Testament again and again: "I was glad when the said to me, 'Let us go to the house of the LORD!.... For the sake of the house of the LORD our God, I will seek your good" (Ps 112). Jerusalem is a holy city, the dwelling and throne of Yahweh (Jer 3:16). This Holy City became the focal point of the messianic kingdom and the center of the worship of Yahweh.

Imagine then the depth of tragedy felt when not only the Holy City but the Temple itself was destroyed. In its long history Jerusalem was attacked many times, but nothing compared to the devastation when it was besieged and stormed under Vespasian and Titus in A.D. 70. In A.D. 69 Vespasian left for Rome, where he was made emperor, leaving his son Titus to carry out the siege of Jerusalem. Titus attacked the city from the northwest and took one wall after another. The fortress Antonia was destroyed, and the whole city was surrounded by a new wall five miles long built to prevent people from escaping.

Added to the horrors of the siege was fighting and killing among factions within the city itself, not to mention the terrible famine that gradually overtook the whole population. Under cover of darkness many tried to flee the carnage but were caught and slit open by Roman soldiers who heard that the terrified Jews had swallowed their gold. Others were crucified until the hills around Jerusalem bristled with thousands of crosses.

Titus had given orders that the Temple—especially the Holy of Holies—should not be burned down, but the soldiers got out of hand, as Josephus narrates in his very detailed account: "The hope of plunder induced many to go on as having this opinion that all the places within the temple were full of money (since they saw) that all around about it was made of gold." They thought the entire Temple was a gigantic treasury house. Josephus continues his description of how

107

Titus tried to prevent the soldiers from destroying this spectacular edifice, but their lust for gold was simply out of control. One of the soldiers "threw fire upon the hinges of the gate, in the dark so [that] flame burst out from within the holy house itself," forcing Titus and his commanders to withdraw. "Thus the holy house burnt down without Caesar's approbation."[17]

Only recently have archaeologists discovered living proof of Jerusalem's burning—a site now visited in the Jewish Quarter called "the burnt house." Apparently the house was the residence of a priestly family, the Bar Kathros clan, at the time of the Jewish revolt. Burnt wood and ashes indicate that the house was destroyed when Titus razed the city. After the burning of the Temple and the lower city, Roman soldiers with drawn swords went through the streets of the upper city and killed anyone they could find, then set fire to their houses. The burnt house was one of those residences.

The rooms of the house, kitchen, and bath were identified by the articles found in them. The numerous finds in the house include a measuring weight with the name "Kathros" on it, a spear, the arm bone of a woman who apparently was struggling to escape from the kitchen. The latest coin found in the debris is dated 69.[18]

The Greco-Roman Impact

As we have seen, to understand the world of Jesus, the region where he grew up, lived his earthly life, and died, one must take into consideration much more than Judaism. Since the time of Pompey and even Alexander the Great in the fourth century B.C., Greco-Roman civilization in the Middle East dominated Palestine. It entered to some degree into every region and phase of life. As Fr. Raymond Brown has put it, "In varying ways and degrees, through commerce, schools and travel, Jews were influenced by a world quite different from that described in much of the Old Testament."[19]

This was sometimes good and sometimes bad. The latter reached its culmination in the siege and complete destruction of Jerusalem and the Temple in A.D. 70. Certainly this was one of the darkest periods in Jewish history, one from which they have never fully recovered. After the annihilation of Jerusalem, the Holy City, especially the Temple where Yahweh's presence was specially honored, Judaism was never the same. No longer could sacrifice be offered, because there was no altar of sacrifice. No longer could pilgrimages be made on feast days such as the Passover, because there was no temple. Christianity also underwent radical change, developing and moving from what seemed at first a Jewish sect into a universal religion, as Paul's mission to the Gentiles graphically illustrates.

At Caesarea Peter Baptizes Cornelius

In Caesarea there was a man named Cornelius, a centurion of the Italian Cohort, as it was called. He was a devout man who feared God with all his household; he gave alms generously to the people and prayed constantly to God. One afternoon at about three o'clock he had a vision in which he clearly saw an angel of God coming in and saying to him, "Cornelius." He stared at him in terror and said, "What is it, Lord?" He answered, "Your prayers and your alms have ascended as a memorial before God. Now send men to Joppa for a certain Simon who is called Peter."...He called two of his slaves and a devout soldier from the ranks of those who served him, and after telling them everything, he sent them to Joppa....Suddenly the men sent by Cornelius appeared [before Peter]....The Spirit said to him, "Look, three men are searching for you. Now get up, go down, and go with them without hesitation; for I have sent them." So Peter went down to the men and said, "I am the one you are looking for; what is the reason for your coming?" They answered, "Cornelius, a centurion, an upright and God-fearing man, who is well spoken of by the whole Jewish nation, was directed by a holy angel to send for you to come to his house and to hear what you have to say." So Peter invited them in and gave them lodging.

The next day he got up and went with them, and some of the believers from Joppa accompanied him. The following day they came to Caesarea. Cornelius was expecting them and had called together his relatives and close friends. On Peter's arrival Cornelius met him, and falling at his feet, worshiped him. But Peter made him get up, saying, "Stand up; I am only a mortal." And as he talked with him, he went in and found that many had assembled; and he said to them, "You yourselves know that it is unlawful for a Jew to be associated with or to visit a Gentile; but God has shown me that I should not call anyone profane or unclean. So when I was sent for, I came without objection. Now may I ask why you sent for me?"

Cornelius replied, "...All of us are here in the presence of God to listen to all that the Lord has commanded you to say."...While Peter was still speaking, the Holy Spirit fell upon all who heard the word....Then Peter said, "Can anyone withhold the water for baptizing these people who have received the Holy Spirit just as we have?" So he ordered them to be baptized in the name of Jesus Christ. (Acts 10:1–48)

Photo by Lorna Patterson

Fig. 36 Remains of Caesarea Maritima. Seagulls wheel and dive over the remains of Herod's famed seaport and political capital on the Mediterranean at Caesarea. Here Peter converted the first Gentile and Paul underwent his long trial and final deportation to Rome as narrated in the Acts of the Apostles.

Photo by Lorna Patterson

Fig. 37 Aqueduct at Caesarea. Depicted are the impressive remains of the aqueduct that brought water from Mount Carmel to Caesarea.

At Caesarea Paul Appeals to Caesar

Three days after Festus had arrived in the province, he went up from Caesarea to Jerusalem where the chief priests and the leaders of the Jews gave him a report against Paul. They appealed to him and requested, as a favor to them against Paul, to have him transferred to Jerusalem. They were, in fact, planning an ambush to kill him along the way. Festus replied that Paul was being kept at Caesarea, and that he himself intended to go there shortly. "So," he said, "let those of you who have the authority come down with me, and if there is anything wrong about the man, let them accuse him."

After he had stayed among them not more than eight or ten days, he went down to Caesarea; the next day he took his seat on the tribunal and ordered Paul to be brought. When he arrived, the Jews who had gone down from Jerusalem surrounded him, bringing many serious charges against him, which they could not prove. Paul said in his defense, "I have in no way committed an offense against the law of the Jews, or against the temple, or against the emperor." But Festus, wishing to do the Jews a favor, asked Paul, "Do you wish to go up to Jerusalem and be tried there before me on these charges?" Paul said, "I am appealing to the emperor's tribunal; this is where I should be tried. I have done no wrong to the Jews, as you very well know. Now if I am in the wrong and have committed something for which I deserve to die, I am not trying to escape death; but if there is nothing to their charges against me, no one can turn me over to them. I appeal to the emperor." Then Festus, after he had conferred with his council, replied, "You have appealed to the emperor; to the emperor you will go." (Acts 25:1–12)

Photo of site sign by Lorna Patterson

Fig. 38 Herod's artificial seaport. Herod's artificial seaport at Caesarea Maritima. Josephus left an account of Herod's reasons for constructing this harbor: "This city is situated in Phoenicia, in the passage by sea to Egypt…and not fit for havens on account of the tempestuous south winds that beat upon them which rolling sands that come from the sea against the shores do not admit of ships….So Herod endeavored to rectify this inconvenience and laid out such a compass towards the land as might be sufficient for a haven wherein the great ships might lie in safety…." (Josephus, Antiquities, 15:331)

Photo by Lorna Patterson

Fig. 39 Dead Sea. Visitors view the Dead Sea to the right from Masada, Herod's palace-fortress, which was the last Jewish stronghold against the Romans until it fell in A.D. 73.

Photo by Lorna Patterson

Fig. 40 Cave #4 at Qumran. At Qumran is Cave #4 in the area where the Dead Sea Scroll discovery was made in 1947. Both sites are on the western shore of the Dead Sea about thirty-five miles apart.

Notes

1. See Bull, Robert J., "Caesarea Maritima: The Search for Herod's City," *Biblical Archaeology Review* 8:3 (1982), 26–41. The author gives an excellent account of archaeological discoveries.

2. Ibid., 26. "According to the first century historian Josephus...the port of Caesarea Maritima was as large as Piraeus, the port of Athens. If so, Caesarea was one of the two or three largest ports in the Mediterranean, indeed in the world."

3. Josephus, Flavius, Wars of the Jews, I:408–15; Antiquities of the Jews, 15:331–41, *The Works of Josephus*, trans. William Whiston, Peabody, Maine: Hendrickson Publisher, Inc. (2000), p. 420. Josephus eloquently describes the marvels of Herod's construction of Caesarea—the size of its seaport, the unique street pattern, and the ingenuity of the sewer system.

4. Murphy-O'Connor, Jerome, O.P., *The Holy Land: An Oxford Archaeological Guide*, New York: Oxford University Press (1998), p. 210.

5. Fitzmyer, Joseph A., S.J., *The Acts of the Apostles*, New York: Doubleday (1998), pp. 453–54. Fitzmyer explains the great importance of this event simply but clearly: "Though this vision is about clean and unclean food, God uses it to prepare Peter for bearing testimony to Gentiles. Cornelius and his pagan household are understood as representatives of such Gentiles. Their acceptance into the Christian church will not formally be recognized until the 'Council' in Ch 15....To guide Peter himself rightly, God's Spirit uses the symbolism of clean and unclean food to teach Peter a proper understanding of Gentiles in the divine plan of salvation. As no food God has provided for his created people can be called unclean, so no human being can be considered unclean, i.e. unworthy of a share in that plan."

6. Ibid., p. 748. In appealing to Caesar, Paul is not immediately sent to Rome. According to Fitzmyer, "Festus has to write a report to accompany him according to Roman law....So the trial of Paul continues, but now in the presence of King Herod Agrippa II and his sister Bernice who have come to greet the new procurator."

7. Ibid., p. 767. With the beginning of chapter 27 Luke begins the story of Paul's transfer from Caesarea Maritima to Rome, where he is to stand trial before Caesar. "His journey has been occasioned by the last declaration of Paul's innocence by Festus the procurator (25:25) and King Agrippa II" (26:31–32).

8. Murphy-O'Connor, *Holy Land*, pp. 2–3. Alexander the Great brought the Middle East under his control in 331 B.C. and died in 323 B.C., leaving his empire to be divided among his generals. Ptolemy received Egypt and Palestine; Seleucus got Syria. Rome's major domination began with the arrival of Roman general Pompey in 63 B.C. Infighting among Jews in Palestine forced the Romans to take charge of the area as a buffer against the Parthians. Herod the Great provided the occasion, as Murphy-O'Connor puts it: "When a strong Romanophile ruler emerged in the person of Herod the Great (37–4 B.C.) they gave him autonomy...."

9. Sepphoris has attracted archaeologists in recent years not only because it was a Greco-Roman city but also because of its proximity to Nazareth. Excavations there are still ongoing. For some of the results, see the articles in *Biblical Archaeology Review* by Batey, Chancey and Meyers, Nitzer and Weiss.

10. Josephus, Wars 2:56.

11. Chancey, Mark, and Meyers, Eric, "How Jewish Was Sepphoris in Jesus' Time?" *Biblical Archaeology Review* 26:4 (2000), 18.

12. Murphy-O'Connor, *Holy Land*, p. 165. The location of this Greco-Roman site makes it obvious why it has been occupied continuously for six thousand years. The tel contains fifteen superimposed cities. The valleys rising from the Jordan gradually merge with the Jezreel Valley running to the coast almost imperceptibly, as Murphy O'Connor has observed: "These valleys have been a trade route from time immemorial and they are controlled by Bet Shean."

13. Grant, F. C., and H. H. Rowley, *Dictionary of the Bible* (2nd ed.), Edinburgh: T & T Clark (1963), p. 267. Living apart in the desert, this so-called monastic community (about 200) refused share in the public services of the temple. The existence of such a sect within Judaism was an extraordinary phenomenon. "Yet the Essenes were Jews in good standing. They were inside, not outside, the pale of strict Judaism. Hence they give the student a problem as interesting as it is difficult."

14. Fitzmyer, Joseph A., S.J., *The Dead Sea Scrolls and Christian Origins*, Grand Rapids, Michigan: William B. Eerdmans Publishing Company (2000), p. I.

15. Originally a fortress-palace of Herod the Great, Masada was captured by the Sicarii, a fanatical sect of Jewish Zealots. This twenty-acre

plateau with sheer cliffs on all sides rose one thousand feet above the Dead Sea—to all appearances an impregnable refuge. Besieged for three years by the Roman army, the Sicarii held out until finally overwhelmed by Rome's tenth legion.

16. Yadin, Yigael, *Masada*, New York: Random House (1966), p. 212. Yadin, director of the Masada excavation, gives his view of Rome's motivation in the conquest of Masada: "What disturbed the tranquility of the Roman Empire were the 960 men, women and children holding out on its summit. Judea had been vanquished. In Rome they had installed their arches of triumph And here, in this place alone...there remained a handful of rebels challenging the entire might of Rome."

17. Josephus, *Wars* 6:266. In graphic detail Josephus has left the following description: "While the holy house was on fire, everything was plundered that came to hand, and ten thousand of those that were caught were slain; nor was there a commiseration of any age, nor any reverence of gravity; but children and old men, and profane persons and priests, were all slain in the same manner; so that this war went around all sorts of men and brought them to destruction as well as those that made supplication for their lives as those that defended themselves by fighting."

18. Murphy-O'Connor, *Holy Land*, p. 74.

19. Brown, Raymond, *Introduction to the New Testament*, New York: Doubleday (1996), p. 64. The social background of the NT makes it necessary to take much more than Judaism into account. For example, Jews bought goods with coins imprinted with Roman gods.

20. Gaster, Theodore H., *The Dead Sea Scriptures*, New York: Doubleday (1964), p. 46.

Chapter 5

THE JEWISH-
CHRISTIAN
CHURCH

Photo by Lorna Patterson

Fig. 41 Steps from Mount Zion to the Garden of Gethsemane. These ancient stone steps go down Mount Zion to the Kidron Valley and the Garden of Gethsemane. Jesus and his apostles may have used them on Thursday night after the Last Supper, which took place on Mount Zion. "When they had sung the hymn, they went out to the Mount of Olives" (Mk 14:26). Then followed the agony in the garden, betrayal by Judas, and the arrest of Jesus, which led to his trial and finally his crucifixion.

Map 11
SACRED SITES IN THE EARLY CHURCH

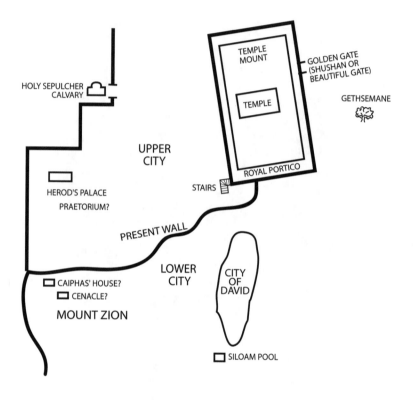

HOLY SEPULCHER
CALVARY

TEMPLE
MOUNT

GOLDEN GATE
(SHUSHAN OR
BEAUTIFUL GATE)

TEMPLE

GETHSEMANE

UPPER
CITY

HEROD'S PALACE

PRAETORIUM?

STAIRS

ROYAL PORTICO

PRESENT WALL

LOWER
CITY

CITY
OF
DAVID

CAIPHAS' HOUSE?

CENACLE?

MOUNT ZION

SILOAM POOL

Sacred Sites in the Early Church

Jesus was a Jew, a fact sometimes not sufficiently appreciated among Christians. He not only was born a Jew but was a Jew in every aspect of his life. As a child he was brought up in the Jewish tradition; and like every Jewish child he first imbibed his Hebrew heritage at his mother's knee. He received a Jewish education, and his parents brought him to Jerusalem regularly on festive occasions.

So likewise were the apostles Jews. As observers of the Torah they followed carefully the prescriptions of the Sabbath. Luke tells us that after the ascension on the Mount of Olives they returned to Jerusalem, which was a Sabbath day's journey away. After entering the city they went to the room upstairs, where the apostles had been staying. Luke gives the names of those who were present: Peter and John, James and Andrew, Philip and Thomas, Bartholomew and Matthew, James, the son of Alpheus, Simon the Zealot, and Judas, the son of James. "All these were constantly devoting themselves to prayer, together with certain women, including Mary, the mother of Jesus, as well as his brothers" (Acts 1:12–14).

Almost from the beginning these first Christians faced persecution. Both Peter and John were called before the Sanhedrin, the highest Jewish court (Acts 4:1–22) and later on, before the high priest (Acts 5:17–42). Individuals in the small community were singled out, such as Stephen, the first Christian martyr (Acts 7:54—8:4). Along with this external persecution, the community had its internal problems as well. One need only to read the graphic story of Ananias and Sapphira and Peter's stinging reproach: "You did not lie to us but to God" (Acts 5:1–11).

Just exactly where all these events took place is not certain. The only site that has been excavated and thoroughly studied is the Church of the Holy Sepulcher. No documentation about the precise location of the sites considered holy has remained. When Jerusalem became a pagan city in A.D. 135 the Roman authorities forbade development of sacred places. In the fourth century, when Christianity could be practiced openly the Christians built churches at various points where they believed the gospel events occurred. For those interested in sacred sites, some things can be said. For instance, the first gathering of the apostles after the ascension was somewhere on the western hill of Jerusalem, the location referred to as Mount Zion.[1]

Other areas likewise can be identified from references given in the Acts of the Apostles. We are told that day by day the apostles and their followers spent much of their time in the Temple, broke bread at home, and ate their food with glad and generous hearts (Acts 2:46). It was in the Temple area that Peter first addressed the assembled Israelites:

> But Peter, standing with the eleven, raised his voice and addressed them, "Men of Judea and all who live in Jerusalem, let this be known to you, and listen to what I say. Indeed, these are not drunk, as you suppose, for it is only nine o'clock in the morning. No, this is what was spoken through the prophet Joel:

> "In the last days it will be, God declares,
> that I will pour out my Spirit upon all flesh,
> and your sons and daughters shall prophesy,
> and your young men shall see visions,
> and your old men shall dream dreams." (Acts 2:14–17)

Thereupon Peter announced that Jesus of Nazareth, confirmed by God with many wonders, rose from the dead as all are witnesses. "Therefore let the entire house of Israel know with certainty that God has made him both Lord and Messiah, this Jesus whom you crucified" (Acts 2:36). When they heard this they were all "cut to the heart" and asked Peter and the apostles, "What shall we do?" Peter's response: Be converted and be baptized. Day by day many continued to be added to their number.

Peter's Healing and the Gate Called Beautiful

Although followers of Jesus, the apostles are portrayed in Acts as devout Jews going up to the Temple for daily prayer. On one occasion Peter and John encountered a man lame from birth begging at the Gate Called Beautiful. "I have no silver or gold," said Peter, "but what I have I give you; in the name of Jesus Christ of Nazareth, stand up and walk" (Acts 3:6). Those in the Temple court were astounded, and word spread quickly.

Just where the Gate Called Beautiful was located at the time of the apostles is not certain. Some scholars identify it with the Golden Gate (or an area beneath it) in the eastern wall of the Old City, just opposite the Mount of Olives. More excavation is needed to clarify the archaeological history of this site. The origin of the gate is obscure, but it is believed that this was the entryway known as Shushan Gate built by Jews returning from the Babylonian exile in the sixth century B.C. In the New Testament this gate may have been the same one Jesus passed through when he entered Jerusalem on Palm Sunday. Before the Crusades it was the point of entry used by religious processions coming into the city.[2]

Various explanations of the Golden Gate have been offered over the centuries by both Jews and Muslims. Among Jews, the gate was considered holy because of a tradition that the messiah would come through it when he entered Jerusalem. To prevent this event from occurring, Muslims not only established a cemetery just outside the portal, but it was also walled up by Saladin in 1187.

Peter Before the Sanhedrin: Solomon's Portico

Inside the Shushan or Golden Gate, Peter and John found themselves in the vast court of the Temple—the courtyard where the entrance to the present Muslim Dome of the Rock now stands. Here they preached with much success, converting so many that they were arrested and cast into prison. The next day they were brought before

Israel's supreme court, most likely assembled in the eastern apse of the portico (also called the Royal Stoa).

Standing before the Sanhedrin, Peter astounded this august body of seventy members with his courage and boldness. Many of them were indeed shaken. A select membership made up of twenty-four priestly classes, this judicial council controlled everything that had to do with religion. The two chief religious parties, the Pharisees and the Sadducees, were present as well. Just who presided is unclear. According to the New Testament and Josephus, it seems that the high priest was in charge at the time of Christ.

The Sanhedrin held court at the east end of the Royal Stoa. Into this impressive and rather hostile setting Peter was brought to defend himself. One approached the huge structure by ascending a stairway over what today is called Robinson's Arch at the southwest corner of the Temple area. The building and the whole width of the Temple Mount from west to east was depicted by Josephus as "more deserving of mention than any under the sun."[3] Built in basilica style, the structure had four rows of columns fifty feet high. Much of it was occupied with various business activities.

Some think that it was from this portico that Jesus drove out the moneychangers and overturned their tables. "My house shall be called the house of prayer but you have made it a den of thieves" (Mt 26:12). Following the miraculous cure of the man lame from birth, Peter and John were most likely brought into this same area in the wake of their arrest. After spending the night in prison, the two apostles were brought to the Temple area and before the Sanhedrin and high priest:

> The next day their rulers, elders, and scribes assembled in Jerusalem, with Annas the high priest, Caiaphas, John, and Alexander, and all who were of the high-priestly family. When they had made the prisoners stand in their midst, they inquired, "By what power or by what name did you do this?" Then Peter, filled with the Holy Spirit, said to them,

"Rulers of the people and elders, if we are questioned today because of a good deed done to someone who was sick and are asked how this man has been healed, let it be known to all of you, and to all the people of Israel, that this man is standing before you in good health by the name of Jesus Christ of Nazareth, whom you crucified, whom God raised from the dead. This Jesus is 'the stone that was rejected by you, the builders; it has become the cornerstone.'

There is salvation in no one else under heaven given among mortals by which we may be saved." (Acts 4:5–12)

The apostles were warned to cease their preaching, which they steadfastly refused to do. Completely frustrated, the Sanhedrin simply threatened them again and let them go. They could find no way to punish them because they feared the reaction of the people. After Peter and John were released, they went to their friends and reported what the chief priests and elders had said. Thus emboldened, the little Jewish-Christian church continued to spread the word in Jerusalem. Besides their activity in the Temple area, Peter and the disciples also continued to assemble in the Upper Room, where the bonds of the Christian community were strengthened (Acts 1:12–14).

The Little Church of God

Such was the very first coming together of the Jewish-Christian community. Where this took place is not absolutely certain, but both history and early Christian writings afford some clues. Traditionally this first gathering was in the same room as the Last Supper, which was also the site of Pentecost. The general location has always been on the western hill of Jerusalem, the region known as Mount Zion outside the walls of the Old City.

This area on the western hill was not destroyed by the Romans, at least not completely, for we know that near here, not far from the present-day Citadel, was the encampment of the tenth Roman legion called Fretensis. From Josephus and others we know that the Roman army attacked Jerusalem from the north, leaving the western hills relatively untouched. After Jerusalem and the Temple were destroyed, Christians who fled to Pella returned to the site of the Upper Room on the western hill. It had been the center around which the first community gathered after the ascension as related by Luke in Acts.[4]

This site would have evoked early memories either from the oldest members themselves or the generation immediately after them. So it is not surprising that early Christian writers speak of a small church constructed on the site believed to be that of the Upper Room or Cenacle. It was called "the little church of God" and is mentioned as such by Bishop Epiphanius, a native Palestinian. Although writing in the fourth century A.D., Epiphanius relied on documents of the second century that described Jerusalem as it was after its destruction. Following the second revolt against Rome in A.D. 135, Emperor Hadrian was determined to build a new Roman city on the ruins of old Jerusalem, a city to be called Aelia Capitolina.

According to Epiphanius, Hadrian found Jerusalem a city completely razed to the ground and "trampled upon," with nothing left standing except a small church of the Christian community. So Roman sources tell us. The bishop adds that this small church was on the site to which the apostles came after the Lord was taken up into heaven, the Cenacle described by Luke in Acts as the "room upstairs."[5]

At the time of Hadrian, this area was outside the city destroyed by the Romans. Returning from Pella about A.D. 130, exiled Christians would have been close enough in time to the first Christian community to remember the location of the Cenacle. Because of the city's vast destruction, access to the area was difficult and full of dangers. Unless a holy place was already revered there by Christians, a new one is not likely to have been built.[6]

From archaeology one might hope to find something to support early Christian testimony about the "little church of God" called the

Cenacle. What one sees today as the Cenacle is not the original building. Rather the interior, which is quite clearly Gothic, dates from the
Middle Ages. One is left then with the possibility that the present edifice was built on the site where the Little Church of God once stood
on Mount Zion. In the fourth century it was known as the Upper
Church of the Apostles. In the fifth century it was called the Mother
of All Churches. Twice the building was burned down.

The present structure was built by the Franciscans in 1335
before they were expelled by Sultan Sulieman the Magnificent in 1523,
the same Turkish emperor who built the walls of Old Jerusalem still
standing today. When complaints were made by Muslims regarding
Christian liturgical processions near the so-called tomb of David,
Sulieman issued a proclamation:

> It is neither just nor appropriate that this more noble place
> (housing David's tomb) remain in the hands of the infidels
> (Christians) and that, in obedience to their impious cus-
> toms, their feet foul the places sanctified by the prophets
> who have a right to our complete veneration. We order then
> upon receipt of this august order, that you expel from the
> church and the convent immediately and without delay the
> religious and all those who reside there.[7]

David, of course, was buried on the eastern hill in Jerusalem (1 Kgs
2:10), but his "tomb" has been incorrectly honored in the same building as that of the Cenacle.

At any rate, the history surrounding the site of the Cenacle and
the area around it presents a montage that can be confusing to modern pilgrims. Beneath the floor of the tomb of David are Crusader,
Byzantine, and Roman floors going back to the second century. There
is no doubt that the region atop Mount Zion contains sites going back
to the origin of Christianity and even before.

Mount Zion: Other Christian Sites

Halfway down the eastern slope of Mount Zion is the Church of St. Peter in Gallicantu (St. Peter at the Crowing of the Cock). Some revere the site as the house of the high priest Caiphas, where Jesus was taken after his arrest in Gethsemane and where Peter denied him three times: "Then Peter remembered the word of the Lord, how he said to him, 'Before the cock crows today, you will deny me three times.' And he went out and wept bitterly" (Lk 22:61–62).[8]

Rock-cut cellars, stables, and a prison lie beneath the house dating from the time of Herod (37 B.C.–A.D. 70). In his *Jerusalem as Jesus Knew It*, John Wilkinson doubts that we have any reliable information about the exact location of this house, though it is reasonable to suppose it was somewhere in the Upper City. At least the site is true to the time period. From this location the visitor has a wonderful view of the Old City nestled between the Hinnom Valley and the Kidron Valley, with the Mount of Olives to the east. Nearby this site begins the ancient stone stairway sloping down from Mount Zion to the pool of Siloam. Some believe that Jesus took this stairway down to the Garden of Gethsemane past the Siloam pool after the Last Supper. Turning left (northward) toward the Zion Gate one sees the tower of the Church of the Dormition. Some believe this site to have been the last resting place of Mary before her assumption into heaven, according the early Christian belief. Others have problems with this location, since tradition holds that Mary spent her final days in Ephesus, where she went with Saint John.[9]

A Sharing and Caring Community

After the first gathering in the Upper Room, the apostles and their followers were engaged in other events in rapid succession. Luke recounts how Peter, the spokesman, directs the reconstitution of the original twelve. Matthias was selected to replace Judas (Acts 1:15–17). Then after the coming of the Holy Spirit, a running picture of the life and trials of this first Christian community emerges. Luke periodically gives brief summaries describing various aspects of early community life. One of those summaries includes a description of how members shared with one another:

> Now the whole group of those who believed were of one heart and soul, and no one claimed private ownership of any possessions, but everything they owned was held in common. With great power the apostles gave their testimony to the resurrection of the Lord Jesus, and great grace was upon them all. There was not a needy person among them, for as many as owned lands or houses sold them and brought the proceeds of what they sold. They laid it at the apostles' feet, and it was distributed to each as any had need. (Acts 4:32–35)

Not only the sharing of goods among themselves but also the doing of good among others is underscored in the accounts of Acts. Many events of healing took place in the Temple area, specifically in the Royal Stoa, which rose above the monumental staircase. Another of Luke's summaries of the Christian community in Jerusalem reveals the result of the community's prayer that God might stretch forth his hand to cure and perform signs and wonders:

> Now many signs and wonders were done among the people through the apostles. And they were all together in Solomon's Portico. None of the rest dared to join them, but the people held them in high esteem. Yet more then ever believers were added to the Lord, great numbers of both men and women, so that they even carried out the sick into the streets, and laid them on cots and mats, in order that Peter's shadow might fall on some of them as he came by. A great number of people also would gather from the

towns around Jerusalem, bringing the sick and those tormented by unclean spirits, and they were all cured. (Acts 5:12–16)

The Challenges of the New Community

The picture of the early Jewish-Christian community portrayed by Luke in Acts in many ways is presented as idealistic, prayerful, equal sharing of community goods, in all things of "one heart and one mind." Aside from external persecution it seemed indeed to be almost flawless—a utopia. In the first period immediately after the ascension, at least, there appeared to be no disagreements. Almost always Peter was at the head of the group as spokesman. He spoke with an authority that all appeared to take for granted. This was consistent with the words of Jesus: "Feed my lambs, feed my sheep." Despite this rather idyllic portrait painted by Luke, the community was not without its inner dissension; after all, it was composed of human beings who were not without flaws. From scriptural evidence and from history, it appears there never was a perfect sinless Christian community—a theme developed by Robert Wilken in *The Myth of Christian Beginnings.* Such is the nature of a church made up of members with free will, which included the possibility, indeed the inevitably, of sinfulness.[10]

One early challenge stands out in contrast to the image of complete peace and harmony. Internal strife developed between the Hellenists and the Hebrews about the distribution of food to widows (Acts 6:1–7). In a male-dominated society, women who had lost their husbands could become victims of abuse and discrimination, which seems to have been the complaint of Greek-speaking Jews called Hellenists. Another group, the Hebrews, spoke a semitic language, either Aramaic or Hebrew. The difference between them seems to have been more linguistic than ethnic. Both groups were Christians, and all were Jews as well. To solve the controversy the apostles came up with a practical solution: "Therefore, friends, select from among yourselves seven men of good standing, full of the Spirit and of wisdom, whom we may appoint to this task" (Acts 6:3). Interesting to note is that those selected all had Greek names—Stephen, Prochorus, Nicanor, Timon, Parmenas, Philip, and Nicolaus—thus assuring a fair food distribution.

Just as Christ appointed twelve to be apostles, so the twelve appointed seven to be deacons. Obviously, as the church grew additional ministers were needed. The word *deacon* employed here (Acts 6:4) gradually came to be used to describe a new category of ministers created by the apostles, who took it for granted that they had the power to do so since they stood in a place of authority over the church. Deacons were subordinate to the apostles, representing an early development in the organization of the fledgling community.

The Church Develops Outside of Jerusalem

As the story of the first Christian community unfolds, we see Peter, John, and the others in the Temple area and still going to the Upper Room on Mount Zion. But gradually their preaching activity began to extend outside Jerusalem and into Samaria, initiating a new phase in the development of the church (Acts 8:5–8).

It was also outside Jerusalem on the road to Damascus that Stephen, one of the newly appointed deacons, gave witness that Jesus indeed was the messiah, resulting in his death by stoning. Stephen's explanation of the Old Testament with Christ as its fulfillment enraged the religious leaders who could not bear his accusation: "Stiffnecked people, uncircumcised in heart and ears, you are forever opposing the Holy Spirit, just as your ancestors used to do" (Acts 7:51). When the crowd stoned him to death, a Jew named Saul approvingly held the clothes of the stone throwers.

Another of the seven chosen as a deacon was Philip, who appeared in Samaria working miracles and preaching. Some Samaritans

Map 12
THE JEWISH-CHRISTIAN CHURCH

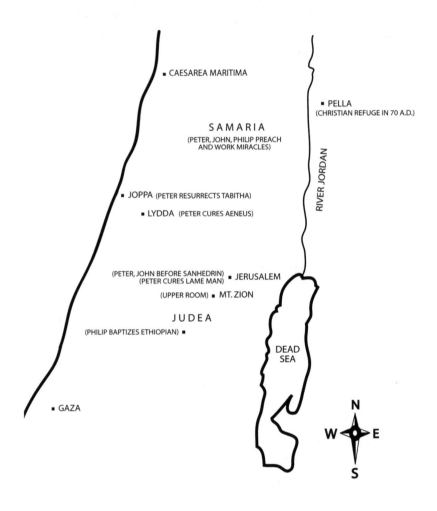

- CAESAREA MARITIMA

- PELLA
(CHRISTIAN REFUGE IN 70 A.D.)

S A M A R I A
(PETER, JOHN, PHILIP PREACH
AND WORK MIRACLES)

RIVER JORDAN

- JOPPA (PETER RESURRECTS TABITHA)
- LYDDA (PETER CURES AENEUS)

(PETER, JOHN BEFORE SANHEDRIN) - JERUSALEM
(PETER CURES LAME MAN)

(UPPER ROOM) - MT. ZION

J U D E A
(PHILIP BAPTIZES ETHIOPIAN) -

DEAD
SEA

- GAZA

N
W E
S

were baptized because of what they heard and saw. When the apostles in Jerusalem became aware of this, they sent Peter and John to confer the Holy Spirit through the laying on of hands.

Later on we find Philip south of Jerusalem on the road to Gaza, near the Mediterranean, where he met an Ethiopian eunuch, a court official of the Queen of the Ethiopians, riding in a chariot. As he traveled he read from the prophet Isaiah about the Suffering Servant (Isa 53). Philip ran up and heard him reading the passage. Philip asked if he understood what he was reading. "How can I?" replies the Ethiopian, "unless someone guides me?" (Acts 8:31). He invited Philip to get in and sit with him. Philip then explains the meaning of the Suffering Servant to him.

> Then Philip began to speak, and, starting with this scripture, he proclaimed to him the good news about Jesus. As they were going along the road, they came to some water; and the eunuch said, "Look, here is water! What is to prevent me from being baptized?" He commanded the chariot to stop, and both of them, Philip and the eunuch, went down into the water, and Philip baptized him. When they came up out of the water, the Spirit of the Lord snatched Philip away; the eunuch saw him no more, and went on his way rejoicing. (Acts 8:35–39)

After that Philip continued on up the Mediterranean coast to Ashdod, past what is now Tel Aviv, and ultimately arrived at Caesarea.

"You Will Be My Witnesses…to the Ends of the Earth"

The activity of Peter, John, and Philip in Judea and Samaria refers back to the main theme of Acts: "You will receive power when the Holy Spirit has come upon you; and you will be my witnesses in Jerusalem, in all Judea and Samaria, and to the ends of the earth" (Acts 1:8).

Expansion of the early church had begun, from Jerusalem to Rome—"to the ends of the Earth."

Likewise, Judea and Samaria relate to Luke's overall Gospel plan—the last journey of Jesus to Jerusalem. The apostles are told not to depart from Jerusalem until they have been clothed with power from on high. "Repentance and forgiveness of sins is to be proclaimed in his name to all nations, beginning from Jerusalem" (Lk 24:47).

Jerusalem remained the center of expansion even when the fledgling church spread to regions outside Israel. This was still the Holy City where Christianity began. Only in Antioch, far to the north, did the "followers of the way," as they were first called, come to be known as Christians. Still, they had to be approved by the apostles in Jerusalem, the most notable example being Paul himself.

Paul was obviously not one of the twelve; his conversion at first was held with suspicion. When he came to Jerusalem and tried to join the disciples they were all afraid of him, this notorious persecutor of the "followers of the way." They did not believe he was a bona fide convert. Paul's Cypriot friend, Barnabas, had some persuading to do: "Barnabas took him, brought him to the apostles, and described for them how on the road he had seen the Lord, who had spoken to him, and how in Damascus he had spoken boldly in the name of Jesus. So he went in and out among them in Jerusalem, speaking boldly in the name of the Lord" (Acts 9:27–28).

And so the church developed from its Jewish-Christian origin deeply rooted in religious tradition to a progression of Christian communities that extended to the Gentiles and even to the center of the civilized world, Rome itself. In Luke's view, it was the action of God working in human history to bring salvation to all nations. It was indeed a community guided by the Spirit, and the spread of the Word itself was likewise the work of the Spirit.

Notes

1. See Fitzmyer, Joseph A., S.J., *The Acts of the Apostles*, New York: Doubleday (1998). An excellent source for sacred sites in the early Jewish-Christian church. This very scholarly work includes Fitzmyer's new translation of Acts as well as an outstanding introduction and commentary. It provided helpful insights throughout this section of my work.

2. See Fleming, James, "The Undiscovered Gate Beneath Jerusalem's Golden Gate," *Biblical Archaeology Review* 9:1 (1983), 24–37. In Greek the word used for "beautiful" is *oraion*, which sounds similar to the Latin word *aurea* meaning "golden." Jerome substituted the latter word for the former so that the Latin vulgate reads "Golden Gate" instead of "Beautiful Gate." The name Golden Gate has been used to this day.

3. Josephus, Flavius, Antiquities of the Jews, 15:413, *The Works of Josephus: New Updated Edition*, trans. William Whiston, Peabody, Maine: Hendrickson Publisher (2000). When Peter appeared in the Royal Stoa before the Sanhedrin he must have been overawed by his surroundings. Josephus seems equally impressed as we see from his description: "This cloister had pillars which stood in four rows...and the thickness of each pillar was such that three men might, with their arms extended, fathom it round, and join their hands again."

4. Hoade Eugene, O.F.M., *Guide to the Holy Land*, Jerusalem: Franciscan Printing Press (1973), p. 305.

5. Ibid., p. 304.

6. Murphy-O'Connor, Jerome, O.P., *The Holy Land: An Archaeological Guide*, New York: Oxford University Press (1998), p. 106. Both tradition and archaeology point to Mount Zion as the site of the Cenacle as far back as the second century A.D. The site became known in the fourth century as the church of God, supported by strong evidence: "It is not impossible that it should have been the 'church of God' mentioned by Epiphanius of Salamis (315–403) as having been in existence on Mount Zion in 130 a.d. Danger and difficulty of access exclude the Christian invention of a new holy place in the 2nd century a.d."

7. Ibid., p. 105. Since the Middle Ages the Franciscans have steadfastly guarded sacred sites in the Holy Land such as Mount Zion even though it meant suffering, death, and expulsion by imperial decree.

8. Ibid., p. 107. The location of the house of the high priest is not certain. Somewhere on Mount Zion is beyond doubt, but the exact site is

disputed. "It is much more likely that the house of the high priest was at the top of the hill; luxurious dwellings of the Herodian period have been found in the Armenian property (just beside the Dormition Abbey) where another house of Caiphas is exhibited."

9. Wilkinson, John, *Jerusalem As Jesus Knew It: Archaeology as Evidence*, London: Thames and Hudson, (1978). p. 132. Actually this site is partway down the hill. Some Christians venerate the site as being the palace of the high priest Caiphas where Jesus was taken after his arrest (Mk 14:53) and where Peter denied Jesus (Mk 14:66–72). However, seventh-century A.D. documentation identifies it as being in the immediate vicinity of the church of Zion.

10. Wilken, Robert, *The Myth of Christian Beginnings*, Notre Dame: Notre Dame Press (1970), p. 158. Luke's picture of the Jewish-Christian church is not entirely idealistic. Besides the evidence in Acts itself, this has been emphasized by such scholars of the early church as Robert Wilken: "The apostolic age is a creation of the Christian imagination. There never was a Golden Age when the church was whole, perfect, pure—virginal. The faith was not purer, the Christians were not braver, the church was not one and undivided."

Appendix I
BIBLICAL SITES AND REFERENCES

Bethlehem
Visitation of the Magi: Matthew 2:1–12
Joseph's dream and the flight into Egypt: Matthew 2:13–15
The Nativity: Luke 2:1–20

Caesarea Maritima
Paul taken prisoner: Acts 23:31–34
Christian message brought by Philip: Acts 8:40; 21:8
Paul's visits: Acts 9:30; 18:22
Conversion of Cornelius: Acts 10:17–48

Capernaum
Jesus taught and healed in the synagogue: Mark 1:21–27
Lowering of a paralyzed man through the roof: Mark 2:1–12
Call of Matthew: Mark 2:13–27
Healing of centurion's servant and Peter's mother-in-law:
    Matthew 8:5–15
Jesus' sermon on the bread of life: John 6:25–59
Pronouncement of judgment on the town: Matthew 11:20–24

Gethsemane
Agony and arrest of Jesus: Matthew 26:36–56
Betrayal and arrest: Mark 14:32–50
Peter's betrayal: Luke 22:39–62
Betrayal and arrest: John 18:1–12

Holy Sepulcher

Jesus is crucified on Golgotha: Mark 15:21–39
Pilate places a guard at the tomb: Matthew 27:62–66
Women find tomb empty: Matthew 28:1–10; Mark 16:1–7;
  Luke 24:1–8
Mary of Magdala mistakes Jesus for gardener: John 20:11–17

Jerusalem

City's conquest by King David; his new capital: 2 Samuel 5:6–9
Building of God's temple by King Solomon: 1 Kings 5–8
Rebuilding of the city and temple after exile: Nehemiah 3; Ezra 3
Visit of Jesus as a boy: Luke 2:41–50
Jesus' triumphal entry, trial, and death outside the city walls:
  Luke 19:28–44
Birth of the church on Pentecost: Acts 2

Nazareth

The Annunciation: Luke 1:26–38
Childhood of Jesus: Luke 2:39–40
Teaching in synagogue: Luke 4:16–21
Jesus reads Isaiah: Luke 4:14–30
Jesus rejected at Nazareth: Matthew 13:54–58

Sea of Galilee

Loaves and fishes: Matthew 14:13–21
Calling of Jesus' first disciples: Matthew 4:18–22
Miraculous catch of fish: Luke 5:1–11
Jesus' calming of the storm: Matthew 8:23–27
Healing of the demoniac: Matthew 8:28–32
Walking on the water: Mark 6:45–52
Jesus' resurrection appearance: John 21:1–14

Tabgha

Multiplication of loaves, Bethsaida: Luke 9:10–17
Feeding of multitude: John 6:1–14; Matthew 14:13–21; 15:32–39;
  Mark 6:30–44; 8:1–10

The Temple Area

Prayer for the peace of Jerusalem: Psalm 122:6–9
Lament for the loss of Jerusalem: Lamentations I
Baby Jesus presented in Temple: Luke 2:21–38
Jesus, aged twelve, questions the teachers: Luke 2:41–50
Satan tempts Jesus: Matthew 4:5–7
Jesus predicts the destruction of the Temple: Mark 13:1–2
Peter and John heal crippled beggar: Acts 3:1–10
Jesus drives traders out of the Temple: Matthew 21:12–13;
    Mark 11:15–17; Luke 19:45–48
Parable of the Pharisee and the tax collector: Luke 18:10–14

Via Dolorosa

Jesus before Pilate: Mark 15:1–21
Jesus betrayed: Matthew 27:1–32
Arrest of Jesus: Luke 22:39–53
Trial and crucifixion: John 18: 28–19:37
Burial of Jesus: John 19:38–42

Appendix II

CHRONOLOGY

Date	Events in Sacred History	World Events
1900 B.C.	Abraham's calling; departure from Ur	King Hammerabi rules Babylon XII Dynasty in Egypt
1800 B.C.	Jacob; Israelites in Egypt; Joseph	Hyksos invade Egypt
1300 B.C.	Exodus: Moses leads Israelites from Egypt Covenant at Sinai Joshua conquers Canaan	Rameses II rules Egypt Trojan War
1200–1000 B.C.	Judges: Deborah, Samuel, Ruth Saul, King of Israel	Phoenician Empire expands Tyre becomes important
1012–975 B.C.	David, King of Israel; Conquest of Jerusalem	Iron Age; Philistines vs. Israelites
975–922 B.C.	Solomon: builds Temple; empire spreads	Hiram, King of Tyre; sends laborers/material for Temple
922–722 B.C.	Kingdom divided: Israel in north; Judah in south	Assyria expands to Mediterranean
	Omri rebuilds Samaria	Foundation of Rome
	Prophets: Amos, Hosea, Isaiah	
722 B.C.	Sargon II conquers Israel	
	Hezekiah: Discovery of Deuteronomy Prophet: Jeremiah	Greek cities develop in Asia Minor
587 B.C.	Fall of Judah; Jerusalem destroyed Babylonian exile; Prophets: Ezekiel, Daniel, Isaiah II	Cyrus the Great conquers Assyrians, solidifies Persian Empire
539 B.C.		Cyrus authorizes return of Israelites

Date	Events in Sacred History	World Events
537 B.C.	Return from exile Palestine becomes part of Persian Empire	
500–400 B.C.	Prophets: Zachariah, Haggai Rebuilding of the Temple Nehemiah rebuilds walls of Jerusalem	Rome conquers Etruscans Darius defeated at Marathon Xerxes defeated at Salamis Parthenon dedicated to Athena Peloponnesian War
400–300 B.C.	End of Persian domination Alexander occupies Palestine 332 B.C. Hellenistic Period	Fall of Persian Empire Alexander's death in 323 B.C.
300–200 B.C.	Palestine controlled by Ptolemies of Egypt	Alexander's empire divided between generals and their descendants: Ptolemies in Egypt and Seleucids in Syria Hannibal and the Punic Wars
200 B.C.	Seleucids take Palestine from Ptolemies Antiochus profanes Temple in Jerusalem	Antiochus II of the Seleucid dynasty destroys Ptolemies' army
165 B.C.	Maccabees retake Temple Hanukkah: Rededication of Temple	
63 B.C.	Conquest of Jerusalem by Pompey	First triumvirate: Pompey, Caesar, Crassus
44 B.C.		Death of Julius Caesar
37– 4 B.C.	Herod the Great Building projects: Caesarea, Masada, Herodium	Second Triumvirate: Octavius, Lepidus, Antony
30 B.C.		Octavius becomes emperor and takes the name Augustus
20 B.C.	Reconstruction of the Temple begins	
6 B.C.?	The birth of Jesus Christ	
A.D. 14		Death of Caesar Augustus Tiberius succeeds
A.D. 26	Pontius Pilate becomes procurator	

Date	Events in Sacred History	World Events
A.D. 27–35	Ministry of John the Baptist	
	Ministry of Jesus	
	Martyrdom of St. John the Baptist	
	Death, resurrection of Jesus	Death of Tiberias
	Pentecost	Caligula succeeds
	Conversion of Paul	Death of Caligula
	Beginning of Gentile mission	Claudius succeeds
A.D. 42	Paul begins his missions	
		Death of Claudius
A.D. 68–70	Christians flee from Jerusalem to Pella	Nero succeeds
	Fall of Jerusalem and Masada	Death of Nero

BIBLIOGRAPHY

Books

Avigad, Nahman, *Discovering Jerusalem.* Thomas Nelson, Inc., New York, 1980.

Bahat, Dan, *The Atlas of Biblical Jerusalem.* Carta, Jerusalem, 1994.

————, Lecture given at the Casa Nova in January 1988

Brown, Raymond, *The Birth of the Messiah,* Doubleday. New York, 1979.

————, *The Critical Meaning of the Bible.* Paulist Press, New York. 1981.

————, *An Introduction to the New Testament.* Doubleday, New York, 1996.

Burri, Rene, *H. V. Morton: In Search of the Holy Land.* Dodd, Mead, New York, 1979.

Buttrick, George (ed.), *The Interpreter's Bible,*Vol. 4. Abingdon Press, New York, 1962.

Charlesworth, James H. and Weaver, Walter P. (eds.), *The Dead Sea Scrolls and the Christian Faith.* Trinity Press International, Harrisburg, 1998.

Fitzmyer, Joseph A., S.J., *The Acts of the Apostles.* Doubleday, New York, 1998.

————, *A Christological Catechism: New Testament Answers.* Paulist Press, New York. 1990.

————, *The Dead Sea Scrolls and Christian Origins.* Eerdmans, Grand Rapids, 2000.

————, *The Gospel According to Luke,* Vols. 1 and 2. Doubleday, New York, 1985.

Gaster, Theodore, *The Dead Sea Scriptures,* Doubleday. New York, 1964.

Gonen, Rivka, *Biblical Holy Places: An Illustrated Guide.* Palphot LTD, Israel, 1987.

Grant, F. C., & Rowley, *Dictionary of the Bible* (2nd ed.). T & T Clark, Edenburgh, 1963.

Hoade, Eugene, O.F.M., *Guide to the Holy Land.* Franciscan Printing Press, Jerusalem, 1973.

Holy Bible, New Revised Standard Version. World Publishing, Iowa Falls, 1997.

Israel Exploration Society, *Jerusalem Revealed: Archaeology in the Holy City— 1968–1974,* Jerusalem, 1975.

Josephus, Flavius, *The Works of Josephus, New Updated Edition,* trans. William Whiston. Hendrickson Publisher, Inc., Peabody, Maine, 2000.

Kenyon, Kathleen, *Digging Up Jerusalem.* Benn, London, 1974.

Loffreda, Stanislao, O.F.M., *Recovering Capernaum.* Franciscan Printing Press, Jerusalem, 1990.

Morton, H. V., *In the Steps of the Master.* Dodd, Mead & Co., New York, 1937.

Murphy-O'Connor, Jerome, O.P., *The Holy Land: An Oxford Archaeological Guide from Earliest Times to 1700.* Oxford University Press, New York, 1998.

Shanks, Hershel, *The City of David: A Guide to Biblical Jerusalem.* Basak Press, Tel Aviv, 1975.

Wilkinson, John, *Jerusalem As Jesus Knew It: Archaeology As Evidence.* Thames and Hudson, London, 1978.

Wilken, Robert, *The Myth of Christian Beginnings.* Notre Dame Press, Notre Dame, 1970.

Yadin, Yigael, *Masada.* Random House, New York, 1966.

Articles: *Biblical Archaeology Review*

Arav, Remi, Freund, Richard A., and Shroder, John F. "Bethsaida Rediscovered," *BAR* 26:1 (2000), 44–56.

Avigad, Nahman, "Jerusalem in Flames—The Burnt House Captures a Moment in Time," *BAR* 9:6 (1983), 66–73.

Bahat, Dan, "Does the Holy Sepulcher Church Mark the Burial of Jesus?" *BAR* 12:3 (1986), 26–45.

Barkay, Gabriel, and Kloner, Amos, "The Garden Tomb: Was Jesus Buried Here?" *BAR* 12:2 (1986), 40–57.

Batey, Richard A., "Sepphoris: An Urban Portrait of Jesus," *BAR* 18:3 (1992), 50–63.

Ben-Yehuda, Nachman, "Where Masada's Defenders Fell," *BAR* 24:6 (1998), 32–36.

Bull, Robert J., "Caesarea Maritima: The Search for Herod's City," *BAR* 8:3 (1982), 26–40.

Chancey, Mark, and Meyers, Eric, "How Jewish Was Sepphoris in Jesus' Time?" *BAR* 26:4 (2000), 18–23.

Fleming, James, "The Undiscovered Gate Beneath Jerusalem's Golden Gate," *BAR* 9:1 (1983), 24–37.

Laughlin, John, "Capernaum from Jesus' Time and After," *BAR* 19:5 (1993), 54–61.

Nitzer, Ehud, and Weiss, Zeev, "New Mosaics at Sepphoris," *BAR* 18:6 (1992), 36–46.

Nun, Mendel, "Ports of Galilee," *BAR* 25:4 (1999), 18–31.

Pixney, Bargil, "Church of the Apostles Found on Mount Zion," *BAR* 16:3 (1990), 16–35.

Ritmeyer, Kathleen, and Ritmeyer, Leen, "Reconstructing Herod's Temple Mount in Jerusalem," *BAR* 15:6 (1989), 23–42.

Shanks, Hershel, "Religious Message of the Bible," *BAR* 12:2 (1986), 58–66.

Shenhave, D., "Loaves and Fishes Mosaic near Sea of Galilee Restored," *BAR* 10:3 (1984), 22–31.

Strange, James, and Shanks, Hershel, "Has the House Where Jesus Stayed in Capernaum Been Found?" *BAR* 8:6 (1982), 26–37.

———, "Synagogue Where Jesus Preached Found at Capernaum," *BAR* 9:6 (1983), 25–55.

Tsafrir, Yoram, "Ancient Churches in the Holy Land," *BAR* 19:5 (1993), 26–39.

Wachsmann, Shelly, "2000-Year-Old Hull Recovered Intact," *BAR* 14:5 (1988), 19–33.

Yeivin, Ze'ev, "Ancient Corazin Comes Back to Life," *BAR* 13:5 (1987), 22–28.